LOKNETE SITARAM GHANDAT (MAMA)

SWAPNIL KHAMKAR

Made with ♥ on the Notion Press Platform
www.notionpress.com

I dedicate this book to my respected parents, teachers, mentors, and all those who guided me, inspired me, and stood by me in my efforts.

But above all, I most sincerely dedicate this book to the esteemed Shri Sitaram "Mama" Ghandat – whose lifelong dedication, tireless efforts, and selfless service have been a constant source of inspiration to me. His work, his thoughts, and his legacy will always remain a guiding force in my life.

Contents

Contents

Foreword

The life of Sitaram "Mama" Ghandat is a testament to the resilience of the human spirit and the power of purposeful leadership. As a figure who rose from the most challenging circumstances to make a lasting impact on his community and beyond, his story deserves to be told, not just as a record of achievements, but as a source of inspiration for generations to come.

This book was born out of a desire to share Mama's journey—his struggles, triumphs, and the values that guided him throughout his life. It is not merely a compilation of facts or a chronological recounting of events. Rather, it is an attempt to understand the essence of a man whose commitment to social welfare and community progress defined his leadership.

In tracing Mama's life from his humble beginnings in Nandur Pathar to his accomplishments as a respected leader and social reformer, I have sought to highlight the qualities that made him unique. His compassion for the underprivileged, his relentless dedication to social causes, and his unyielding belief in unity and progress are themes that resonate throughout this biography.

The purpose of this book is not to glorify a man or elevate him beyond his humanity. Rather, it is to illuminate how an individual, born into adversity, can rise to prominence by embracing empathy, integrity, and the tireless pursuit of justice. Mama's story demonstrates that leadership is not about power or prestige, but about serving people and uplifting those who have been marginalized.

As you read through these pages, you will encounter a man who was far from perfect, yet remarkably principled. Mama's journey was shaped by his own experiences of poverty, discrimination, and hardship. But rather than allowing these struggles to define him, he used them as motivation to forge a better path for himself and others.

The task of documenting such a rich and multifaceted life has been both challenging and rewarding. I have relied on interviews, historical records, personal testimonies, and Mama's own reflections to present an account that is both honest and engaging. This book is intended for anyone who seeks inspiration from real-life examples of courage, perseverance, and selfless service.

It is my hope that this biography will not only inform but also inspire. That it will encourage readers to reflect on their own potential to contribute positively to society. And that it will honor the legacy of a man who dedicated his life to the welfare of others.

With deep respect and admiration for the life of Sitaram "Mama" Ghandat, I present this book as a respect to his enduring legacy.

Sanjay Khamkar

Acknowledgements

Writing this book has been a journey of deep admiration and gratitude. It is not only a tribute to the life of Sitaram "Mama" Ghandat but also a reflection of the countless people who have been part of his journey. This work would not have been possible without the support, guidance, and inspiration of many individuals.

I am immensely grateful to all those who shared their experiences and insights about Mama's life. Family members, friends, colleagues, and community members who provided valuable memories and perspectives have been instrumental in shaping this biography. Their kindness and cooperation are deeply appreciated.

Special thanks to those who offered their time for interviews and shared personal anecdotes, which brought depth and authenticity to this work. Their voices have added richness to the narrative and helped paint a more complete picture of Mama's life.

I also wish to express my gratitude to those who encouraged and supported this project from its inception. Their faith in the importance of sharing Mama's story has been a constant source of motivation.

Finally, my deepest appreciation goes to Mama himself. His life's journey serves as an inspiration not only to those who knew him personally but to all who seek to make a positive difference in the world. This book is dedicated to preserving his legacy and ensuring that his story continues to inspire generations to come.

With heartfelt gratitude,
Swapnil Khamkar

CHAPTER ONE

THE JOURNEY OF AN EXTRAORDINARY MAN

Sitaram "Mama" Ghandat's life story is a profound testament to the power of human perseverance and the unbreakable spirit that can emerge from humble beginnings. His remarkable journey—from modest origins to becoming a respected public figure—has inspired countless individuals who face obstacles in their own paths. This book aims to share his life in a way that is both simple and moving, illustrating that true leadership does not require privilege or wealth. Instead, it is built on determination, the desire to serve others, and a steadfast belief in the possibility of change. In the chapters that follow, you will encounter a man who remained grounded in his values despite climbing to positions of influence, and who worked tirelessly to uplift people around him. This introduction offers a glimpse of who Sitaram "Mama" Ghandat is, why his life is so significant, and how his story sheds light on broader themes of endurance, social progress, and inclusive leadership.

From a distance, Mama's story might appear similar to that of many people who move to a big city in search of better opportunities. Yet, as you look closer, you see a life propelled by both adversity and hope. Even in his early years, Sitaram "Mama"

Ghandat demonstrated a combination of curiosity and determination that hinted at the leader he would become. Though he lacked many basic resources, and though educational opportunities were scarce, he refused to let his circumstances define him. Instead, he chose to define his circumstances, often crafting his own chances where none seemed to exist. This unwavering commitment to self-improvement was the first step on a winding road that would lead him to prominent positions in politics and social work.

One of the most striking qualities about Mama is his genuine sense of empathy. All too often, personal struggle can instill bitterness or cynicism in a person. However, for Mama, those trials became the springboard for service. He recognized, from a young age, that hardship and inequality affected not only him but also countless others who lacked a supportive platform. Gradually, this realization shaped his entire perspective. Whether someone needed support for education, access to clean water, or a voice in local governance, Mama sought to provide real solutions. He understood how important it was to help others overcome limitations, because he himself had faced many barriers before finding the path to self-determination. Over time, this approach developed into an unshakable philosophy: When one individual thrives, entire communities benefit.

His life also underscores a vital element of leadership—resilience. Making the journey from a cramped living area to the Maharashtra State Legislative Assembly was not straightforward or easy. Mama encountered repeated setbacks, faced skepticism from those who saw him as "unqualified," and fought against longstanding prejudices. Yet, time and time again, he refused to yield. A natural sense of optimism and a practical willingness to put in extra effort became his signature response whenever doors closed in front of him. If a job opportunity required skills he did not have, he would learn those skills—sometimes by practicing all night long, or by seeking out mentors. If a powerful figure tried to silence his viewpoints, he would strive to persuade them with sincerity and logic. If the public was unconvinced of his capacity to deliver, he would campaign tirelessly from morning to night, showing them in person what he was capable of achieving. These moments, repeated countless times, molded him into a dynamic figure who could adapt to almost any situation, always returning stronger and wiser.

This biography will show that his strength did not revolve solely around personal ambition. Instead, what truly fuels Mama's achievements is his sense of responsibility to the community. He does not measure success only by votes earned or titles acquired. Rather, he measures it by the number of households that gain clean water, students who attend new schools, roads that become safer for travelers, and families who no longer worry about basic necessities. Throughout his career, Mama connected with people of various castes, religions, and classes, recognizing the value each person brought to the community. This inclusive spirit became a hallmark of his political and social endeavors. In an age where divisions and disagreements often overshadow cooperation, Mama's conviction that unity drives progress offers a refreshing and practical lesson in leadership.

In writing this book, we must ask: why is Sitaram "Mama" Ghandat's story so important to share? The simplest answer is that it embodies hope. Across the world, countless individuals struggle with feelings of despair when they face discrimination or poverty. They may feel alone in the face of daunting circumstances—financial constraints, limited education, or systematic inequalities. Mama's life stands as a bright example that one does not need to be born into privilege to make a lasting impact. His story shows that even with minimal formal education, a person can rise to influential roles when driven by sincerity and consistent effort. Rather than allow others' expectations to weigh him down, Mama capitalized on every chance to learn, train, and uplift. He used each position—be it a humble job or a high-profile role—to advance social welfare, focusing on policies and projects that directly assisted the underprivileged.

Another crucial aspect of his journey is the moral lessons it offers. So often, success stories highlight competition, individual accolades, and personal glory. While Mama did experience recognition in various spheres—political, social, and personal—he consistently pointed that recognition back to the communities and networks supporting him. Whether in grassroots mobilization or large-scale development projects, Mama remembered the difficulties he faced in his youth. He did not forget what it felt like to worry about housing or face the uncertainty of unemployment. Because of this, empathy remained the centerpiece of his leadership style. Through good times and bad, he retained a sense of humility that endeared him to the very people who voted him into office or entrusted him with leadership roles in cooperative institutions.

It is also worth noting how Mama navigated the complexities of politics. Politics, especially at local and state levels, can be a demanding arena where alliances shift, rivalries intensify, and personal ambition can cloud a person's original intentions. Despite these pressures, Mama managed to keep his priorities clear. He aimed to represent people's needs: rural infrastructure, better educational opportunities, and fair assistance to the poor. His successes in these areas are not minor footnotes. In fact, they underline how an authentic connection with constituents can lead to real, on-the-ground improvements. The significance of those contributions resonates not merely in an official record of achievements, but in the everyday lives of individuals who witnessed tangible changes—like smoother roads, more reliable water supplies, and better chances for children to learn and grow.

In personal and social terms, Mama also stands out as a role model who broke barriers in thought and action. In many societies, individuals from marginalized groups continue to be discouraged from aspiring to positions of influence. Mama's life reaffirms that one's background or social label does not dictate their potential or define their future. By confronting prejudice with courage and responding to challenges with renewed vigor, he forged a path that others can now follow. Each time he succeeded, he proved that perseverance wins over doubt, that the willingness to learn can make up for formal degrees, and that sincere service builds deeper trust than any fancy credentials could. Such lessons remain universally relevant, transcending geography and time.

Moreover, no introduction to Mama's life would be complete without acknowledging his flair for connecting with everyday people. In an era of complicated political jargon and flashy media campaigns, Mama's style of reaching out was often simple and personal. He would hold direct meetings, talk openly, and listen attentively. People in the community felt comfortable approaching him, whether they were laborers, small farmers, or struggling shopkeepers. This genuine approach fostered a culture of respect—he respected them, and in turn, they respected him. By earning their trust, he was able to enact ideas and programs that directly addressed their most pressing concerns. This community-focused method, grounded in personal relationships, underscores the value of local engagement in driving lasting development.

Though Mama's story does highlight many accolades, such as positions held and recognition from influential figures, these accomplishments did not occur in a vacuum. They emerged from consistent hard work, a refusal to give up when confronted with seemingly insurmountable barriers, and the ability to inspire others to share in a collective mission. For Mama, each new milestone was not just about personal triumph; it was about validating the hopes of the people who had placed their faith in him. Even in the face of criticism or defeat, he clung to the idea that every end is simply a chance at a fresh beginning. This mindset propelled him forward, constantly searching for ways to deliver better services and create meaningful solutions for everyday struggles.

As readers embark on this biography, it is important to understand the spirit in which it has been written. This book does not aim to lionize an individual or make him appear flawless. Like anyone else, Sitaram "Mama" Ghandat is human, with imperfections and moments of self-doubt. He encountered misunderstandings, made hard decisions that not everyone agreed with, and shouldered the responsibility for outcomes that shaped entire communities. Yet, it is precisely these imperfections that make his story universal and relatable. When we see him wrestle with doubt or overcome roadblocks, we see a reflection of the challenges we might confront in our own lives. Each chapter is a journey through successes, failures, lessons learned, and the spirit of never giving up.

The purpose here, in essence, is to bring forward an authentic narrative that can resonate with anyone who has ever faced setbacks. By sharing how Mama navigated the labyrinth of societal and political structures, the book hopes to empower readers to look at their own circumstances differently. If Mama could surmount those odds—beginning in a disadvantaged setting and eventually channeling his energy into initiatives that benefitted large populations—then perhaps we, too, can cultivate that same determination within ourselves. The story does not promise that the road will be simple; on the contrary, it will reveal the many difficulties and heartbreaks that come with charting one's path. Still, the overarching message is one of hope, showing that positive transformation is possible.

Throughout the pages that follow, you will get a sense of Mama's major accomplishments that demonstrate his influence in political, social, and personal realms. Politically, he navigated multiple roles, even becoming an independent MLA, which underscored his deep community ties and broad appeal across party lines. Socially, he championed various causes—expanding educational access, improving infrastructure, and promoting communal harmony. On a personal level, his growth from a young boy with restricted chances to a recognized leader in Maharashtra exemplifies what is achievable when persistence meets purpose.

Thus, this biography seeks to do more than simply document facts and timelines. It is an invitation to witness how conviction, compassion, and consistent action can merge to form a life story that transcends traditional barriers. Each chapter will unfold with honesty, focusing on distinct phases in Mama's life and aspects of his legacy. By the end, readers should have a clear understanding not only of the man himself but also of the broader social setting that enabled him to flourish. The introduction you are reading now stands as the foundation—an opening window into a world shaped by a singular personality who refused to accept that life had to be as limiting as it first appeared.

Mama's entire ethos was rooted in reaching people from every walk of life, whether they were scholars or day laborers. Writing this story in a plain, heartfelt style respects that ethos, ensuring that all readers can appreciate the significance of his message. His work was never restricted to an elite audience; it was for families who struggled to pay for their children's education, for small business owners who needed a helping hand, and for individuals who yearned to break free from the cycle of poverty.

In summing up the essence of Sitaram "Mama" Ghandat's life, we see a tapestry woven from countless small acts of service, personal sacrifices, triumphant breakthroughs, and unwavering moral codes. What emerges is not just a portrait of one man but an example of how a single person's determination can reshape the destiny of many. This possibility—that good leadership is capable of catalyzing broad social change—remains an inspiring beacon, especially in a world still grappling with economic disparities and deeply rooted social injustices. Through Mama's endeavors, we learn that leadership is not confined to speeches or ceremonies; it is cultivated in day-to-day interactions, in straightforward problem-solving, and in an enduring commitment to fairness.

By the close of this book, my hope is that readers of all backgrounds will find motivation in Mama's journey. I hope this story energizes young students who doubt whether their limited finances can stop them from dreaming big, small-scale entrepreneurs who want to uplift their communities, and seasoned professionals searching for renewed purpose in public service. Indeed, the spirit that propels Mama's life is a universal one: a willingness to try, fail, and try again, combined with compassion for people from every walk of life.

In the chapters ahead, we will explore many dimensions of Mama's experiences. We will discover how he overcame educational barriers, formed alliances in politics, and found creative ways to fund projects that expanded the possibilities for those living on the margins. We will also see how his personality—humble yet driven—shaped his interactions with everyone he met. Yet this introduction stands as the heartbeat of the biography, capturing the fundamental reasons why Mama's story is worth telling in detail. He exemplifies what a person can achieve by balancing ambition with altruism, intelligence with sincerity, and power with humility. The seeds of these qualities were planted early in life, blossoming over time into the extraordinary story that this book aims to share.

And so, we begin. The pages that follow will not only celebrate Sitaram "Mama" Ghandat's life but also shed light on the many ways he sparked transformation in his surroundings. Like a guiding torch, his experiences illuminate a path that others can follow, reminding us that progress is not the domain of the privileged alone. Instead, it can be sparked by anyone who believes passionately in the worth of every individual and works tirelessly to ensure no one is left behind. That belief is the crowning jewel of Mama's legacy, and it sets the tone for the remarkable chapters yet to come.

ROOTED IN RURAL INDIA: FAMILY AND EARLY BACKGROUND

Sitaram "Mama" Ghandat's life began in the rugged hills of Nandur Pathar, a small village in Ahmednagar district. This village, like many others in the region, was isolated by rough roads and limited resources. Mama was born into a Chambhar (SC) family, a community traditionally associated with shoe repair and related leather work. From the moment of his birth, he was immersed in a world shaped by caste hierarchies, economic struggles, and the relentless quest for survival. Though he would later become well-known for achievements that took him far from his birthplace, the foundation of his character and values was laid in this environment of scarcity and resilience.

In rural Maharashtra, during the time of Mama's birth, society largely functioned on a system of caste-based occupations. Each group or "jati" was historically assigned specific types of labor—some held land, some practiced weaving, others farmed, and still others served as barbers or potters. In the Chambhar community, the customary role was to mend or produce footwear.

Mama's father worked diligently as a cobbler in the village, repairing chappals and shoes for local farmers who relied heavily on foot travel over dusty roads and fields. There was rarely a day off—if shoes were torn, they needed fixing promptly, and villagers expected the work to be done quickly and cheaply. Payment often came in the form of food or small sums of money, leaving little room for financial security.

At the heart of this family was Mama's father, a man bound by his occupation but determined to provide for his children. Despite his best efforts, consistent income was a challenge. The family owned no farmland, meaning there was no reliable harvest they could call their own. In places like Nandur Pathar, farmland was a key to stability—it provided both grain to eat and a potential surplus to sell. Without that land, Mama's household was constantly vulnerable to droughts, economic shifts, and the ever-changing goodwill of the village. If the farmers themselves faced difficult times, so did families like Mama's, who depended on them for odd jobs and scraps of grain.

Mama's mother, Radha Bai, was an equally important figure in the household. She was known around Nandur Pathar and neighboring villages for an eye medicine she created. The remedy was a simple handmade mixture of ingredients such as chuna (lime) and bilboa, reputed to soothe sore eyes in just a couple of days. Though she sold it at only a small price—one anna for a tiny box—this modest income often helped the family buy necessities like jaggery, grains, or cooking oil. Neighbors and travelers from several villages would sometimes visit just to obtain this helpful medicine. In many ways, this activity foreshadowed Mama's later realization that small, consistent efforts could become a lifeline for those in need.

Despite these attempts to supplement the family's meager earnings, life remained arduous. Gathering fuel for cooking was a daily task. Children in the family would collect wood to feed the chul, a traditional stove fueled by sticks and twigs. The smell of smoke would fill their modest living space every morning and evening. While most families in the area struggled in some shape or form, not everyone faced the same depth of hardship. Owning land, even a small patch, often meant security. Yet for Mama's family, the lack of land was a constant reminder of how precarious their livelihood was. There were days when the main meal consisted of bhakri and tea sweetened with jaggery instead of sugar.

Growing up with two older brothers, Dagadu and Babu, and three sisters, Kondabai, Yashodabai, and Baghabai. Mama's older siblings sometimes performed small tasks around the village or helped their father with cobbler work to secure a bit more food or a few more coins.

The extended family dynamic was woven into the tapestry of life in Nandur Pathar. Houses were small, usually built of mud walls and thatched roofs. Relatives might occasionally share living quarters if they fell on harder times or passed through the village. Yet there was a quiet strength in these communal living arrangements. Strong family ties meant that if someone fell ill or needed help in the fields, others would do their best to step in. This sense of familial unity forged a tight social network that, while not wealthy, proved resilient in the face of adversity.

Still, Mama's father had only limited means to protect his children from the broader social framework that discriminated against their caste. Society's emphasis on occupation-based hierarchy meant that Mama's family was viewed by some as "lower" and undeserving of the same rights or resources as those from "higher" castes. For instance, when it came to formal education, children like Mama and his older siblings were often not allowed to sit inside the classroom with other students. Instead, if they did attend, they might have to sit outside on sacks or a rough floor, listening to lessons through the doorway. This exclusion, while painful, was considered the norm in many rural areas.

The caste-based system also influenced the family's social interactions. Though individual villagers might occasionally be kind or appreciative—especially if they needed shoes repaired—many still clung to age-old prejudices. For a young child, encountering such bias left a deep impression. It taught Mama from an early age that the world could be unfair, but it also drove him to question why such boundaries existed at all. He saw his father and mother working tirelessly, demonstrating honesty and skill, yet they remained economically and socially vulnerable. Such contradictions planted seeds of empathy and reflection within him, even if he had not yet found the words to articulate them.

At home, the children had to learn self-reliance quickly. For instance, if one sibling fell sick, the others would gather around to help draw water from the well, prepare simple meals, or fetch more wood for the stove. Clothing was scarce, often passed down multiple times. Mama might wear a shirt that once belonged to his older brothers, patched and resewn by his mother to ensure it lasted as long as possible. Shoes, ironically, were a luxury even though the family mended them for a living; often the children went barefoot, their soles hardened by years of walking on dirt roads.

The village environment also offered some moments of genuine community. On certain occasions—festivals or marriages—everyone would come together, regardless of caste, to celebrate. People would share what little they had: homemade sweets, traditional songs, or religious festivities. It was in these brief episodes of collective happiness that Mama witnessed the potential for unity. If only the prejudices and barriers could be dismantled, perhaps life in Nandur Pathar might not feel so harsh. Even as a child, he had a keen eye for noticing how small acts of kindness could bring people closer.

Nevertheless, the realities of prejudice often overshadowed such glimpses of harmony. On rare occasions, when Mama would manage to attend a local school, he felt the weight of stigma from fellow students. They might tease him for smelling of leather or for having so little to eat at lunch break. Even teachers, who were supposed to be role models, sometimes treated students differently based on their caste background.

These experiences were not merely personal burdens; they influenced the entire family's sense of identity. Mama's father likely remembered a time when his grandfather and great-grandfather had occupied the same role, following the same trade of shoe-making. Unlike some trades that allowed for upward mobility, the occupation was tightly bound by social norms, creating a cycle that was difficult to escape. In many rural regions of India, people born into the SC communities faced structural barriers that seemed almost insurmountable. They were often denied access to higher education, government jobs, or entrepreneurial opportunities that might allow them to break free from generational poverty.

Yet, Mama's mother refused to succumb entirely to these limitations. Her medicinal eye balm provided a sense of autonomy. She might have lacked formal credentials, but she possessed valuable knowledge, turning everyday materials into a remedy that villagers appreciated. This small entrepreneurial spirit showed that there were ways to improve one's lot, even within a restrictive social framework. Over time, people traveled from other villages—some even 10 or 20 kilometers away—seeking her treatment. While it did not make them wealthy, it offered a glimpse of a different way forward: harnessing one's abilities and resourcefulness to build a modest but necessary service.

Within the family circle, Mama also began to show signs of curiosity. He would occasionally watch how his mother made the medicine, measuring out the lime, mixing it into a paste, and carefully scooping it into small boxes. Later, he might ask his father why people with sore eyes seemed so relieved after just a couple of applications. Although he was only a child, he was already learning that knowledge, even of a basic home remedy, could be a powerful thing. This early exposure to hands-on work would shape his perspective on what it meant to be productive and useful in a community.

The family composition itself—three sons, three daughters, plus two parents—meant that resources were stretched thin. Each sibling had a distinct personality, but collectively, they formed a support system. Family became aware that survival might require venturing beyond the village. Meanwhile, older brothers might assist in the shoe-repair business when the father had too many orders to complete alone. The younger sisters usually helped their mother around the home, collecting water, grinding grains, or aiding with meal preparation.

Despite having a large family, Mama's household did not escape the challenges of food insecurity. On days when villagers had no shoes to repair or lacked money to pay, Mama's father might earn nothing at all. In such instances, the mother would rely on leftover grain—often bajri (millet)—gifted by local farmers who remembered that the Ghandat family had done them a favor at some point. This reliance on the goodwill of others was always uncertain. Sometimes Mama and his siblings would go to bed with only a bare minimum in their bellies, haunted by an empty feeling that gnawed at them through the night.

Yet even with these hardships, the family maintained a sense of dignity. Mama's parents tried their best to instill in their children the importance of honesty, diligence, and mutual care. Their philosophy was that although times were hard, one must never betray the trust of the community or neglect the needs of neighbors. That emphasis on moral fortitude would later become a key factor in Mama's worldview. His father, despite working within the constraints of the caste, took pride in doing his job well. If the farmer's shoe or sandal needed stitching, he would ensure the work was strong enough to last through many days of walking across rough terrain. If the mother's eye medicine was supposed to heal, she would never compromise on quality or cheat customers with inferior mixes.

The rural backdrop of Nandur Pathar also introduced Mama to the cycles of nature that dominated agricultural life. Even though his family had no farmland, the changing seasons affected the availability of shoe-repair work. During planting and harvest seasons, villagers were busier in the fields, meaning fewer people brought footwear to mend. Conversely, after monsoons, shoes were often damaged by mud and rain, so Mama's father might see a small uptick in repairs. Through these cycles, the importance of farmland loomed large: had Mama's father owned even a small plot, the family would have had a more dependable source of food and income.

In a broader sense, these formative years left an imprint that would guide Mama in later stages of his life. By directly experiencing the sting of social exclusion, the fragility of income, and the power of small but innovative ideas (like his mother's medicine), he internalized lessons that textbooks never taught. His early environment showed him both the harsh realities of a stratified society and the potential for modest improvements through creativity and collaboration.

Above all, Mama's childhood exemplified how early struggles shape character. Though he was still young, he had observed his father laboring under the hot sun or by a dim lamp, stitching shoes far into the evening hours. He had seen his mother, her eyes strained from mixing medicine, greeting visitors with a hopeful smile. He had accompanied siblings on endless walks to gather wood or fetch water, a daily demonstration of how survival in rural settings required constant effort. All these moments combined to form a robust inner core in Mama. Even if circumstances often felt dire, there was always a flicker of determination and resourcefulness.

That flicker illuminated Mama's understanding of what it meant to be "rooted in rural India." It was not just a location or a set of beliefs—it was an entire way of life shaped by land, labor, and social expectation. Being rooted meant you carried both the soil under your feet and the burdens of your community in your heart. It meant you learned to confront prejudice by building relationships rather than retreating. It meant you respected the dignity of work, whether that labor was recognized or looked down upon by others.

Mama's family ties kept him connected to these values. His parents' resilience resonated through the everyday responsibilities they fulfilled without complaint. His siblings supported each other in small but meaningful ways—fixing a torn shirt, sharing the last of a handful of roasted grains, or giving comfort when someone fell ill. Even extended family members, though not always present under the same roof, contributed to a network of shared survival strategies.

As Mama grew, the interplay between harsh circumstances and quiet defiance—defiance of a system that wished to keep him in a place of subordination—became more pronounced. While he was not yet old enough to thoroughly analyze caste-based oppression or economic injustice, he understood that some families had more than enough, while his had barely enough to get by. He recognized that some children in the village attended school daily, wearing neat uniforms and writing in notebooks, while he and his siblings sometimes sat outside with ragged clothes. Such observations lit the first sparks of determination in Mama's mind: the idea that change was possible, even if he did not know yet how to make that change happen.

Thus, the chapter of his life rooted in rural India stands as a powerful prelude to all that would follow. He was shaped by more than just poverty; he was shaped by a collective sense of resilience, moral guidance from hard-working parents, and a community that oscillated between prejudice and generosity. If Mama later chose paths that broke caste barriers or overcame educational limits, it was because he had once experienced, firsthand, the frustrations of being denied opportunities. If he later dedicated himself to helping others, it was because he learned the impact of small acts of kindness, like a mother's homemade medicine that soothed the eyes of the ailing.

Throughout these early years, Mama remained a child at heart—curious, eager, sometimes mischievous. The intense bond that came from sharing the same difficulties helped him to see that collective progress often begins within the family. Before one can lead a community, one must understand the daily struggles and dreams that define its existence.

Looking back, it is clear that Mama's birthplace and childhood environment were pivotal in forming his outlook. Nandur Pathar, for all its challenges, was the training ground where he observed the interplay between tradition and adaptation. He gleaned from it the importance of never underestimating a person's ability to innovate under pressure. He learned that empathy must be practical, providing tangible help to those in need, whether that meant stitching shoes or formulating a cure for sore eyes.

In essence, Mama's early life in Ahmednagar district is a story of raw resilience buttressed by family and community ties. Rooted firmly in the earth of rural India, guided by a caste-defined occupation that was limiting, Mama began to see that hardship need not be permanent. Even as a child, he sensed that one can aspire to a world bigger than the one handed down through birth. Step by step, day by day, he gathered experiences that would serve as the building blocks for his future. And while he did not yet realize it, these lessons of perseverance, community upliftment, and unwavering willpower would soon propel him beyond the horizons of Nandur Pathar.

Thus concludes the tale of Mama's family and early background—a time of many trials, but also a time in which the seeds of his future leadership were quietly sown. The story of rootlessness, or lack of property and social privilege, became the foundation on which Mama would build a life of greater possibility and compassion. One day, he would reflect upon these memories, grateful for how they shaped him. The next steps of his journey would take him away from his rural birthplace, but the values and lessons of home would remain with him always, guiding his path forward.

CHAPTER THREE

CHILDHOOD STRUGGLES AND DAILY LIFE

Sitaram "Mama" Ghandat's childhood was shaped by the hardscrabble reality of village life, where each day brought new challenges and small victories. Early on, he understood that his family's survival depended on a delicate balance of hard work. Growing up in a setting with limited resources, Mama experienced firsthand the constant need to adapt. He learned how to navigate social barriers, assist his parents as they struggled to make ends meet, and occasionally indulge in small acts of mischief that hinted at his future creativity and determination. This chapter explores those childhood struggles and the daily rhythms that defined his early life, revealing the seeds of strength and resourcefulness that would guide him into adulthood.

In Mama's village, the lines between survival and hunger were perilously thin. Nearly everyone knew the pangs of scarcity, but families like Mama's, who had no farmland or stable income, felt it most intensely. Because there was rarely enough money in his household, Mama's parents often depended on goodwill within the community. For instance, a local farmer might offer them a small quantity of millet if Mama's mother gave one of her homemade remedies for sore eyes. Sometimes, another villager would share leftover vegetable scraps in return for a favor—perhaps the repair of a well-worn pair of sandals. These exchanges were never grand gestures, but each one meant that Mama's siblings and parents would have another meal or enough grain to last a few more days.

The entire atmosphere in the village supported this form of reciprocal charity. Housewives trading spices, children borrowing each other's clothes, or neighbors donating extra firewood to a struggling family—all these acts served as an informal safety net for those living on the margins. Yet, for Mama's household, it was not always guaranteed. If the harvest was poor one season, the farmers themselves barely had enough to feed their own families, let alone spare any for others. In these times, desperation overshadowed the typical spirit of generosity, and Mama learned the painful lesson that even acts of kindness depended on the uncertain fortunes of rural life.

Despite these uncertainties, Mama's parents did their best to maintain dignity. They never demanded charity outright; instead, they offered what little service they could. Mama's father might mend a villager's torn footwear or perform small tasks around the village. His mother sold her eye balm in tiny boxes for a single coin. The family's hope was that by giving something in return—be it a product or a labor service—they could receive essential supplies without losing their sense of self-respect. In many ways, this approach taught Mama that humility and resilience often walk side by side: you learn to ask for help when it is needed, but you also strive to contribute what you can, however modest.

Over time, Mama became acutely aware of how precarious his family's situation was. He recognized that on days when the shoe repair work was scarce or when fewer people needed eye medicine, the family's ability to eat depended heavily on donated rations. He observed the worry etched into his parents' faces whenever they tried to stretch their last handful of millet or rice. For a child, such moments could be frightening, but they also ignited a spark of motivation. Even before he fully understood the world, Mama felt an urge to lighten his parents' burden someday—to somehow alter the cycle of need that governed their daily lives.

Even as the family worked to secure basic necessities, Mama faced another formidable challenge: the caste discrimination that permeated everyday life in the village. Like many children from marginalized castes, he was not permitted to sit inside the classroom with his peers. Instead, he had to remain outside, perched on a rough gunny sack in the corridor or near an open window. From there, he strained to hear the teacher's lessons and watch demonstrations on a blackboard he could scarcely see. This scenario was humiliating and confusing for any young mind. Despite having the same curiosity and eagerness to learn as other children, Mama was forced to occupy a physical and social space that underscored his "otherness."

The experience left emotional scars. Children often long for acceptance, for a sense of belonging among classmates. Yet, the school environment reminded Mama of the persistent boundaries that divided the community. While some children teased him outright, others simply avoided him out of ignorance or fear of breaking unwritten social rules. Even the teacher's attitude ranged from reluctant tolerance to outright dismissal. On days of severe weather—blazing heat or torrential rain—Mama found little comfort in the meager shelter outside the school's main hall. The structure might have a tin roof overhang, but no one truly cared whether the child on the sack was getting wet or sweating uncomfortably in the afternoon sun.

However, Mama's determination proved stronger than these indignities. He listened intently, trying his best to memorize whatever he could from the snippets of lessons he overheard. If he managed to catch a glimpse of what was written on the board, he would practice forming letters in the dirt later, using a small stick in place of chalk. Occasionally, a sympathetic teacher or classmate might give him an old, tattered book. The pages could be torn or dirty, but Mama valued each page as if it were a treasure. Late in the evening, he might show these borrowed lessons to his older siblings or his mother, hoping to piece together the knowledge that had so often been denied to him during formal classes.

This exclusion from the classroom did more than hinder Mama's academic progress—it stirred in him a deep sense of injustice. Why, he wondered, should any child be made to sit outside, away from proper desks and chalkboards? Why should a person's chance to learn be dictated by a label attached to their birth? Although he was too young to articulate a protest, the seeds of future activism and empathy were sown in those early days on the sack. For now, his strategy was simple: endure the discrimination, gather as much knowledge as possible through any means, and keep alive the desire to learn, no matter the barriers.

Taken together, the experiences of living on village charity, sitting outside the classroom, relying on his mother's homemade medicines for survival, and occasionally succumbing to mischief shaped Mama's worldview. His daily life was filled with subtle lessons that would follow him all the way through adulthood.

The physical layout of his home was equally modest, reinforcing how little space existed between the family and the harsh realities outside. A single room might double as a kitchen, dining area, and sleeping space at night. The roof was often made of simple thatch or occasionally tin sheets, which rattled loudly under the force of monsoon rains. Each day started early, with Mama's mother preparing a small meal if enough supplies were available. She might fry a bit of grain or make a thin porridge. Once morning chores were done, Mama either attempted to attend school—knowing he would sit outside—or stayed back to help with errands like fetching water from the well.

Throughout the day, Mama might run small tasks for the family: collecting firewood along the edges of the nearby fields, picking up messages from neighbors, or searching for any opportunity to earn a single coin. The streets were dusty, dotted with potholes, and during the rainy season, they turned into muddy channels that made movement difficult. Still, Mama's bare feet grew used to these conditions, and he learned to navigate them without complaint. His acceptance of the environment did not mean he saw it as fixed; rather, he simply recognized that complaining about mud or dust would not change the fact that it was the only home he knew.

Evenings were spent in dim lamplight, the glow of a small oil lamp revealing the family's tired faces. Conversations often centered around practical concerns: What would they eat the following day? Could Mama's father find enough shoe-repair work to buy a little cooking oil or jaggery? Mama listened keenly, absorbing every detail. Though he was not yet old enough to contribute significant income, his presence in these discussions allowed him to understand the complexities of running a household with very few resources.

Despite the daily hardships, the family found moments of joy. Sometimes, a friendly neighbor who received successful treatment for sore eyes might repay the kindness by bringing sweet treats or fresh vegetables from their field. On a rare festival day, Mama and his siblings could watch a village performance of folk dances or drama. These glimpses of festivity and community warmth balanced the rigors of day-to-day survival, reminding Mama that life could hold more than just struggle.

The interplay between adversity and small acts of relief made Mama sensitive to other people's difficulties. Just as his mother's medicine treated the pain in someone's eyes, Mama saw how small gestures of help—like returning a lost goat or offering a handful of grain—could ease the burdens others carried. This understanding was less about formal morality and more about empathy born of shared hardship. It was no grand philosophy, but a simple truth hammered in by hunger, thirst, if you can help, you do, because you understand what it means to go without.

It was in these subtle yet profound ways that Mama's childhood hardships shaped the person he was becoming. Each facet of daily life, from how he obtained his meager education to the way he occasionally filched one anna, taught him resilience and perspective. The precariousness of his family's finances forced him to think creatively and remain vigilant for opportunities. The discriminatory attitudes at school lit a fire within him to prove that he was every bit as capable as the children who sat inside. And watching villagers benefit from his mother's small remedies showed that true value can come from the simplest products, so long as they genuinely meet a need.

As he approached adolescence, the restlessness in Mama's mind grew. He dreamed of scenarios where poverty did not dictate each day, where a child could sit in a classroom free of bias, and where families could rely on something more stable than charity alone. These thoughts were still unformed, swirling in the background of his mind, but they were strong enough to plant a sense of longing in him. At times, he would peer down the dusty road leading out of the village, wondering what lay beyond the horizon. Perhaps in cities or in other parts of the district, life was different. Perhaps there were places where no one had to beg for grains or fear that tomorrow's meal might not come.

Nevertheless, Mama did not allow these daydreams to blind him to the immediate needs of the present. He still woke up each morning to the same thin walls and the same uncertain store of flour or millet in the house. He still faced an uncertain welcome at school. Yet, instead of becoming bitter, he used these conditions as motivation. By observing how swiftly small acts of help could change someone's day, Mama began to piece together an understanding of how vital community bonds could be. And by acknowledging that a single anna was enough to buy a bit of happiness or feed someone for a day, he learned the monumental difference even small resources can make when placed in the right hands.

These childhood experiences laid a crucial groundwork. Mama learned that survival requires both cooperation and self-initiative. In the everyday struggles for food and water, he observed how a community might come together—or fail to—depending on circumstances. In education, he recognized that discrimination could force him to learn in unconventional ways, prompting him to find knowledge wherever he could get it. Through his mother's medicinal skills, he discovered that even in a humble household, there could be a spark of entrepreneurship, an ability to earn and care for others simultaneously. Finally, through his moments of mischief, he gleaned that while seizing small opportunities might bring temporary joy, nothing replaced the sense of security that came from honest, stable means.

Mama's resourcefulness, born out of necessity, would follow him as he eventually ventured beyond the village. Though this chapter focuses on his childhood, it foreshadows the adult who would one day tackle social disparities and infrastructural deficiencies with the same determination he once applied to eavesdropping on classroom lessons. In the grand tapestry of his life, these early years represent the threads of resilience, adaptability, and empathy—qualities that would later mark him as a leader who understood how the smallest interventions could yield transformative results.

CHAPTER FOUR

SEEDS OF AMBITION: LIMITED SCHOOLING

For many children growing up in rural settings, education is both a lifeline and a struggle. The idea of schooling promises an escape from generational poverty, yet for countless families, economic hardships and limited local facilities make extended education seem more like a luxury than a basic right. This tension was especially visible in the early life of Sitaram "Mama" Ghandat, whose schooling ended abruptly after the 4th standard—the highest level available in his village. Although the circumstances at the time prevented him from pursuing formal studies any further, they also planted a restless determination in his heart. In this chapter, we explore how that short-lived schooling shaped his worldview and fueled the ambitions that would eventually propel him to seek broader opportunities in life.

In Mama's village, the school building was modest: a few small classrooms, teachers juggling multiple grade levels, and a courtyard that served as a playground on rare, carefree afternoons. Officially, the curriculum extended only to the 4th standard. Beyond that, there were no additional classrooms or instructors qualified to teach higher grades. Once students completed their primary schooling, their educational trajectory largely hinged on whether they could travel to a nearby town—or, for the more fortunate, enroll in a distant city school.

For most families in the area, the concept of finishing even these four grades was considered a minor victory. Many children dropped out much earlier, pressed into household chores, fieldwork, or other tasks necessary for survival. In Mama's own home, there was a lingering hope that he might be the one to continue further, to study long enough to secure a job beyond the confines of the traditional caste occupation. Still, the village's limited offerings meant that, even for the most enthusiastic student, there was simply no structured path forward once they reached the 4th standard exam.

That limitation weighed heavily on children who were curious and eager to learn. Mama, who had already discovered a keen sense of observation, realized the school's resources were simply insufficient. By the time he reached the 4th standard, teachers were already discussing how they lacked the capacity to open a 5th standard class. He watched older boys drift away from education and into manual labor or small crafts as soon as they finished primary school. Though Mama did manage to complete all the years offered, he knew that his academic journey was on the verge of an abrupt and disappointing conclusion.

Despite the brevity of his education, Mama had experienced enough of the classroom to recognize its value. Though his lessons were often overshadowed by scarce materials and the stigma that came from social prejudice, he found sparks of genuine enlightenment in school. He learned to read simple Marathi texts, which opened his world to basic stories and moral lessons. He was introduced to arithmetic, able to add and subtract small sums—an invaluable skill for someone whose family often juggled finances by the coin. Even the chance to recite poems or prayers in front of classmates, though at times anxiety-inducing, gave him a small sense of self-expression.

It was these small joys that made him crave more. Often, after school hours, he would take his textbooks home, reading the same passages repeatedly until the printed words were nearly etched in his mind. If he stumbled across an unfamiliar term, he tried to ask friends or neighbors for clarification. Sometimes, a traveling vendor or a distant relative visiting from Mumbai provided new insights, a new word, or a glimpse into a larger world beyond the horizon. Such encounters intensified his hunger for knowledge, making him question why it had to stop at the 4th standard.

In addition, Mama grasped that formal learning could help break certain cycles of hardship. If he learned to read and write effectively, he might one day navigate government paperwork on behalf of his family or earn a job that did not rely solely on physical labor. Village elders, accustomed to the old ways, might have seen this as wishful thinking. But Mama, in his youthful optimism, perceived in every written page a doorway to possibilities—better jobs, higher respect in the community, and a voice in local affairs.

Sadly, ambition does not always align with material circumstances. For Mama's parents, daily survival took precedence over distant possibilities. With scarce land and inconsistent income, the family had limited financial flexibility. Traveling to a nearby town for secondary education—perhaps 10 or 15 kilometers away—meant daily transport expenses or lodging costs if the child had to stay near the school. Neither option was feasible for a household that sometimes struggled to afford basic groceries.

Even if Mama's parents had wanted to gather the money, the day-to-day uncertainties of their shoe-repair work left them with no safety net. One poor harvest or a stretch of reduced cobbler business could undermine any savings they painstakingly built up. Under these conditions, sending Mama away for further studies seemed like an impossible gamble. There was no guarantee that the investment would pay off, especially when the family needed every spare rupee just to make it through the month.

Moreover, the household chores that Mama contributed to—fetching water, gathering firewood, and occasionally helping his father with manual tasks—were critical. Losing his labor to the pursuit of further education would place extra strain on his parents and siblings. In a situation where every small act of help made a tangible difference, the idea of sending a child away for schooling was more than just a financial hurdle; it threatened the delicate balance of survival. For Mama, this realization was a bitter pill. The very love that nurtured him also bound him to a routine of responsibilities that left little room for extended academic exploration.

Beyond money, distance formed another major obstacle. Even if Mama's family scraped together the funds for a bus or a bicycle, the road to the nearest higher-grade school was neither easy nor safe. The region's infrastructure was basic—unpaved roads, sporadic public transport, and no dependable system of daily commutes for students. Stories circulated about children who tried to travel, only to drop out when the journey became too taxing or expensive. Some families arranged accommodations with distant relatives or friends in nearby towns, but that option still entailed costs for food and lodging, not to mention the emotional toll of being separated from loved ones.

For Mama's parents, the thought of sending their youngest child to live in a strange town was daunting. They worried about his safety, especially given that they could not afford to visit frequently or check on his well-being. If any medical emergency arose or if the caretaker's promises proved hollow, Mama might end up stranded or worse. Although staying in the village severely limited his educational prospects, it offered familiarity and the security of having family close by.

As a child standing on the edge of the only world he knew, Mama felt a deep yearning to explore life beyond the constraints of the village. Yet, at the same time, he was faced with the emotional pull of home, where he understood the daily rhythms and found the loyalty and comfort of family. This internal tension—between the longing to expand his horizons and the necessity of remaining where he was needed—defined much of his adolescence.

The abrupt end to Mama's formal schooling might seem like an unfortunate twist in his life's story. However, it also set the stage for the grit and creativity that would become his trademarks later on. Having tasted the value of education yet being unable to pursue it fully, Mama grew determined to seek knowledge elsewhere. He paid attention to everyday experiences, gleaning lessons from roadside conversations, religious gatherings, and any reading material he could borrow. In the process, he cultivated a flexible mindset. Lacking a structured academic path, he learned to improvise.

Mama sharpened his observational skills by noticing how different trades worked, how village elders resolved disputes, and how traveling merchants or visitors from the city carried themselves. This attentiveness later helped him adapt quickly when he migrated to Mumbai. Knowing that he could not depend on a formal institution for advanced learning, he pushed himself to become a self-starter. Whether it was practicing letters in the sand or doing mental math while helping with family finances, he turned daily life into an ongoing classroom. Rejection or disappointment, especially about schooling, could have led to despair. Instead, Mama used it as motivation, telling himself that if the village could not offer him more, perhaps somewhere else would. This attitude of hope—combined with realism—anchored him when he encountered bigger trials in the future.

Ultimately, the frustration of having his schooling capped at 4th standard fueled his ambition like few other experiences could. Deprived of a conventional route toward success, Mama became convinced that he would find another path, even if he had to create it himself. This conviction, though nascent in his youth, gave him an inner drive that many with more extensive schooling sometimes lacked.

Despite being unable to continue his studies formally, Mama did not let that fact define his potential. The greatest gift those 4th-standard lessons gave him was the ability to read and write at a basic level. With that foundation, he could at least interpret signage, read simple instructions, and keep basic records. These skills might seem minimal by modern standards, but in a rural environment where literacy rates were low, they were significant.

Eager to apply this knowledge, Mama sometimes assisted neighbors in writing letters or filling out simple forms—tasks that many older villagers struggled with. In doing so, he earned small tokens of gratitude: a handful of grain, a piece of cloth, or simply a heartfelt thank you. More importantly, these interactions revealed how literacy could bridge gaps between ordinary people and the bureaucratic structures that governed land titles, ration cards, and public welfare schemes. Mama began to glimpse the power of documentation: whoever could fill out forms and navigate official processes gained a certain advantage.

In daydreams, Mama imagined a life where he could do more than just read and write at a basic level. Perhaps, if he had the chance, he would learn English, the language used in government offices and city businesses. Or perhaps he would enroll in a training program that could qualify him for some specialized trade. These fantasies were tied to the idea that beyond the dusty roads of his village, there existed an entire world of opportunity—one that was currently out of reach. Even though Mama had only a hazy sense of what that world entailed, the very existence of it stirred in him a quiet resolve to keep moving forward.

A sobering part of Mama's adolescence was watching certain peers leave the village to continue their education elsewhere. Often, these individuals came from slightly better-off families—maybe they owned a small patch of farmland, or they had relatives in the city who could accommodate them. Every so often, Mama would learn that one of these acquaintances had passed their 7th or 10th standard exams in a nearby town. Some even moved to larger cities to study up to the 12th standard or beyond. Their stories filtered back through letters or word of mouth, often accompanied by tales of new experiences—seeing tall buildings, riding a local train for the first time, or encountering a life less tethered by old traditions.

Mama took particular interest in these stories, peppering returnees with questions whenever they visited. What subjects did they study? How did they afford room and board? Did they miss home? Most of all, he wanted to know whether this education was truly transforming their futures. Though some youths complained about cramped lodgings or the hustle of city life, many expressed the excitement of learning new things and expanding their horizons. Their achievements, however minor, felt like signals that a larger world was indeed accessible to those daring enough to claim it.

Yet, with each inspiring success story came the inevitable pang of recognition that Mama's family lacked the resources to send him down the same path. While listening to these travelers' tales, he might feign casual interest, but inside, he felt a spark of envy and longing. He would return to his daily chores with a sense of yearning, clinging to a hope that one day he, too, could escape the constraints of a 4th-standard education.

Mama's predicament was not unique; it mirrored the struggles of many children in his village and neighboring hamlets. Their families were poor or landless, their schooling ended abruptly, and their future seemed to revolve around manual labor or menial tasks dictated by social status. This collective experience sometimes fostered resignation: a belief that their caste-defined occupation was the only route available. But for a few individuals—Mama among them—this adversity became the very spur that propelled them to dream of something more.

In hushed conversations under starlit skies, some young villagers would talk about moving to Mumbai or Pune, cities reputed for their factories and mills. Others pinned their hopes on learning a skill or trade, maybe tailoring or carpentry, which might fetch a better wage than toiling in the fields. Though these discussions were mostly speculative, they revealed that Mama was not alone in his dissatisfaction. A small but determined undercurrent of ambition ran through the community, nurtured by the universal desire for dignity and upward mobility.

Despite their limited means, Mama's parents did not dismiss his aspirations. They saw how eagerly he had pursued the scant education available and how strongly he yearned for more. Though they never explicitly told him he could not continue studying, their silence on the topic spoke volumes: they simply did not have the resources to make it happen.

In many ways, these unspoken regrets strengthened Mama's resolve. If he couldn't continue at that time, perhaps he could find another route later. He did not blame his parents; on the contrary, he empathized with the burdens they carried. Instead, the constraints imposed by their poverty acted like a silent nudge, encouraging him to one day create better conditions for himself—and maybe even for others who shared a similar plight.

These formative years, marked by academic stagnation and financial impossibility, did not stunt Mama's growth as a person. Rather, they redirected him toward a self-directed path of learning. In the short term, he did not have the resources to attend a higher school, but he could still glean insights from everyday life. He asked older villagers about agricultural techniques, curious about how rainfall and sowing seasons worked, even though his family did not own land. He listened intently when travelers described city markets, gleaning whatever information he could about how goods were bought and sold.

In doing so, Mama gradually cultivated a broad, practical understanding of the world. While formal curriculum would have taught him structured lessons, his real-life inquiries taught him adaptability and inventive thinking. He made mental comparisons between village practices and the glimpses of modernity he heard about, piecing together an image of a society that was larger and more complex than the one he knew. Over time, this exposure would become valuable ammunition for his future pursuits, whether in business, politics, or community service.

Although Mama could not map out every step of his journey at this stage, he carried in his heart a quiet pledge: to find or forge a path beyond what the village offered. Each day he spent performing monotonous chores, each moment he felt the sting of not having opportunities that others took for granted, reinforced his determination. He would say to himself that someday, somehow, he would step outside these confines.

And indeed, this sense of unfinished educational business would shadow him for years. In times of hardship, he recalled how close he had come to continued studies and yet how far. The memory fueled his willingness to take risks, experiment with new jobs, and migrate if necessary. It also helped him empathize with children he would later encounter who faced their own truncated educations. Mama's life eventually took him down roads that were quite distant from the village school of his boyhood, but he never forgot that sense of longing to learn and the frustration of being cut off just as he was beginning to grasp the potential of academics.

In reflecting on this chapter of Mama's life, it becomes clear that limitations in formal education did not limit his spirit. Instead, they set the stage for a different kind of learning—a learning anchored in real-world observation, relentless curiosity, and resilience in the face of adversity. His inability to go beyond the 4th standard was a tremendous obstacle, but it also planted in him the seeds of ambition and shaped the kind of leader he would become. He learned that knowledge, in its many forms, could be acquired through nontraditional routes. Most importantly, he discovered that a lack of conventional credentials does not have to define a person's destiny.

Though Mama did not immediately have a solution to the problem of limited schooling, the dissatisfaction it caused never left him. It rippled through his choices—when he decided to migrate to bigger cities, seek small jobs, or mingle with influential people who might teach him something new. In the grand narrative of his life, these constraints were not a dead end; they were a detour, albeit a painful one, that introduced him to a broader understanding of how the world can be both unjust and full of hidden potential.

By the end of his 4th standard year, Mama was no longer just a boy confined by his circumstances. He was a budding thinker, already searching for a way out of the village's educational vacuum. The frustration of seeing no direct path forward fueled an inner fire—one that would guide him to seek opportunities wherever they might appear. This chapter highlights not just the challenges he faced, but the foundation of his lifelong quest to better himself and, ultimately, to uplift others who stood at the crossroads of hope and limitation.

In the chapters yet to come, we will see how Mama carries this determination into the wider world, transforming the same yearning for education into a more profound thirst for progress. The seeds of ambition that sprouted during these early days would, in time, blossom into a relentless drive to foster development and social justice, ensuring that younger generations would not have to suffer the same academic roadblocks he did. For now, however, Mama remained at a standstill, an adolescent boy with a mind brimming with questions, longing to burst free from the tiny boundaries of his village school. The 4th standard might have been the final level on paper, but in Mama's heart, the journey toward knowledge and opportunity was only just beginning.

CHAPTER FIVE

FIRST STEPS TO MUMBAI: HOPES AND REALITIES (1950s)

When a young Sitaram "Mama" Ghandat decided to leave his village for Mumbai in the 1950s, he was both excited and apprehensive. At home, he had faced unyielding challenges—caste discrimination, scarce schooling options, and family poverty. The city held out the promise of something different: perhaps a steady job, or a chance to break away from the traditional cobbler's life. Though Mama did not entirely know what lay ahead, he was fueled by the hope that he could make a living and, in some way, alter the course of his life.

This chapter traces Mama's earliest experiences in Mumbai—the heartbreak of crowded slum life, the uncertainty of sleeping on the street, and the hard grind of shoe polishing for meager earnings. It highlights the resiliency he developed and the relationships he formed, even in these toughest of circumstances.

For Mama, who had watched his parents struggle to feed their many children, the prospect of working in a big city was thrilling. Although he knew life there could be harsh, the possibility of earning even a modest but steady income was appealing. He imagined returning to his village one day with money to repair his parents' rickety home, or enough to provide for his younger siblings in times of need. That vision kept him determined and emboldened him to take the journey.

Traveling to Mumbai required considerable effort and a bit of borrowed money. Mama boarded a train, likely from a nearby town, feeling both awe and anxiety. The train ride itself was a novelty—he had never before sat in a clattering carriage that weaved through stations, stopping at towns he had never heard of. Occasionally, vendors would pass, selling tea or savory snacks. Mama had limited funds, so he resisted the temptation to spend, clutching his small bundle of belongings and imagining the city that waited at the end of the line.

When Mama stepped off the train at one of Mumbai's central stations, he was greeted by an overwhelming crush of people—commuters hurrying to offices, hawkers selling newspapers, and porters weaving through crowds. Towering buildings dwarfed him at every turn. The roads were a cacophony of tram bells, car horns, and constant chatter. All around him, the city pulsed with a frenetic energy completely different from the stillness of his village.

Initially, Mama hoped to stay with Kondabai, imagining that they would share a cramped room but at least have each other's company. However, he soon discovered that her chawl room in Kala Chowki's Ambewadi was already overflowing. With two daughters, a son, and her husband, Kondabai had just enough space for her immediate family. There was no separate corner for Mama—no bed, no spare cot, not even enough floor space to unroll a mat. Although she cared for her younger brother, circumstances prevented them from living under the same roof.

Out of options, Mama realized he would have to find his own place to sleep. Yet, as a newcomer with no stable job, he had neither the contacts nor the money to rent a room or even share one with strangers. Night was closing in, and Mama found himself wandering the streets, clutching a small cloth bundle with a change of clothes and a thin blanket.

It was then that he discovered an unlikely refuge: Bus Stop No. 44 in Kala Chowki. This stop, like many in Mumbai, offered a makeshift covering—a little shelter intended to protect passengers from the sun and rain. Late at night, however, no buses ran frequently, and very few people lingered about. Mama spread out his bedding on the hard pavement, using his bundle as a pillow, and tried to sleep amid the roar of passing vehicles and the city's constant hum. A friend named Raghunath Gawali, who was also in search of a place to rest, shared this meager space. In time, Mama grew accustomed to the routine: arriving at the bus stop after sundown, keeping his few possessions close, and waking at dawn before the daily commuters arrived.

Life sleeping on the street was precarious. Mama found himself worrying about thieves or the occasional police patrol that might ask him to move. It was during these uncertain days that he encountered a flower seller who worked in the same area. The man operated a small stall of fresh garlands and loose flowers, typically used in religious offerings or as décor for weddings and festive occasions. His stall stayed open late into the night, illuminated by a dim bulb connected to a nearby power line.

Over a few conversations, the flower seller took a liking to Mama's polite demeanor and earnest spirit. Perhaps he recognized the same desperation in Mama's eyes that he once felt when he first arrived in Mumbai. Though the flower seller had no spare room to offer, he did suggest a bit of help: Mama could store his thin bedding and blanket behind the stall each morning. This way, Mama wouldn't have to carry it around all day, an exhausting and sometimes dangerous prospect in a city crowded with pickpockets and hustlers. It also meant that Mama had a small patch of ground near the stall where he could lie down at night without being directly on the sidewalk or bus stop bench.

That small gesture changed the texture of Mama's life. No longer worried that someone would steal his bedding while he searched for work, he felt a spark of gratitude that eased the sting of homelessness. Each morning, he would fold his bedding neatly and tuck it behind the stall. In exchange, he offered to fetch tea for the flower seller or help carry the heavy flower baskets from the supplier's truck. It was an informal arrangement—no rent, no contract—just one struggling man helping another who was struggling a bit more.

In a city as vast as Mumbai, such acts of compassion stood out. While many people lived hurried lives, focusing on their own survival, the flower seller's kindness was a reminder that even strangers could become allies. Mama grew even more determined to find stable work, so he could eventually repay this generosity and, perhaps, secure a roof of his own.

Despite having left the village with hopes of finding a steady job, Mama quickly discovered that opportunities in Mumbai were not as plentiful or as easy as he had imagined. Hundreds of new arrivals poured into the city every day, flooding the informal labor market. With limited education—he had only finished up to the 4th standard—and no specialized skills beyond cobbler work, Mama struggled to compete. Still, he refused to give in to despair, waking up at sunrise each morning to scour the nearby neighborhoods for any lead.

One of the city's main hubs in that era was the Crawford Market. It opened around 6:00 AM, bustling with traders bringing in fresh produce, grains, and other goods to distribute across the city. Mama noticed that many of these traders and shopkeepers wore shoes that became dusty or muddy from the back alleys and storage units. Figuring he could make use of his background in shoe work, he approached them with a simple offer: shoe polishing and minor repairs for a few coins. Some responded positively, appreciating the service before they started their busy trading day.

The pay was paltry—maybe just enough to buy a modest meal—but it was something. Mama, however, did not limit himself to the wholesale market alone. Later in the morning, he would wander into the area near Zaveri Bazaar, known for its gold shops and jewelry businesses. This was a more affluent zone, and he hoped to polish shoes for wealthier customers who might pay a bit more. Sometimes, the shop owners—busy tending to clients—would allow Mama inside to work on shoes that customers had left for cleaning. Other times, he would stand on the pavement outside, calling out to passersby in the hope that they would stop for a quick polish.

The earnings, though meager, at least gave Mama a degree of independence. By around 10:00 AM, he would have earned a few coins, enough to buy a plate of vada pav or a cup of milky chai. If he was lucky, he could stretch his income to cover a simple dinner as well. Yet there were days of utter disappointment too. Sometimes, no one seemed interested in getting their shoes polished, or business was too slow, leaving Mama with barely enough to buy a small snack. These were the moments that tested his spirit—when an entire day of pacing the streets resulted in next to nothing.

After about two to two-and-a-half years of this unsettled existence, Mama felt torn. He had migrated to Mumbai with dreams of a better life, but instead found himself sleeping by a flower stall and toiling for pocket change. He reflected on his siblings' decisions. One brother eventually found work in a textile mill. Another stayed in the village, making or repairing shoes on a small scale. Meanwhile, Mama had pinned his hopes on the city, only to face relentless uncertainty.

Despite the obstacles, Mama's resilience did not waver. Each night, he returned to the flower stall, stored his bedding, and shared a few words with the vendor who had shown him kindness. On certain days, Mama would help transport flower baskets from trucks, earning a small tip. On others, he would wander through side streets offering shoe polishing to random office workers during their lunch breaks. In many ways, this tireless hustle foreshadowed Mama's future. He did not wait for opportunity to knock; he chased it down every alley, even if it meant countless rejections or repetitive tasks.

Amid the hustle of daily life, Mama caught fleeting glimpses of a better future. Sometimes, when a kindly customer gave him a few extra coins as a tip, he would savor the prospect of someday earning more and paying for his own room—a tiny space he could call his own. Occasionally, he would pass by buildings with signs indicating government offices or bank headquarters. Seeing men in neat uniforms or crisp shirts brought a wave of admiration, stirring a longing in Mama that went well beyond shoe polishing. He was under no illusions; his limited education and background put such jobs well out of reach. Yet, somewhere in his mind, the notion took shape that a government position—or at least a more stable occupation—might secure him a life free from sleeping on the streets.

Another source of hope came from observing the city's unstoppable growth. The roaring mills, the jam-packed markets, and the constant influx of people pointed to a metropolis that never really slept. If such explosive development was possible in one place, Mama reasoned, perhaps there was room for people of all backgrounds to carve out a living. True, inequality was stark—wealthy people shopped in glittering bazaars while he barely earned enough to cover meals. But the sheer scale of Mumbai's economy suggested that if he persevered, an opportunity might arise.

As the weeks turned into months, Mama got to know more people in the Kala Chowki. This settlement was a maze of narrow lanes, corrugated tin roofs, and makeshift houses built from tar sheets or salvaged wood. Water taps were few, and lines for the communal toilets often stretched endlessly. Here, Mama encountered a different kind of community life—one that was raw and harsh, yet bound together by shared misfortune and small acts of mutual aid. Everyone was hustling for daily survival, whether by selling vegetables, fishing in the nearby docks, or picking rags to sell for recycling. Despite constant struggles, there was a certain camaraderie in the area.

Occasionally, Mama considered trying to rent a corner of a shack with others, but the tiny sums he earned from polishing shoes made it financially out of reach. Sharing even the most dilapidated space required money for deposit and monthly rent. Many slum dwellers formed close networks based on regional ties—some had migrated from the same districts or spoke the same dialect. Mama, relatively new to this environment, did not have a longstanding circle of hometown acquaintances to vouch for him. Yet, his friendly nature and willingness to help gradually earned him a place in the informal community, even if he remained on the periphery.

This period, filled with adversity, served as a crucible for Mama's character. Sleeping on bus stops and behind a flower stall tested his resolve, but it also taught him invaluable lessons about city life and human resilience. He saw how strangers in a metropolis could exhibit both extreme indifference and sudden generosity. One day, a person might walk by without even glancing at him; the next day, someone might buy him a cup of tea just because they felt a pang of sympathy. In this ever-shifting urban landscape, Mama learned to appreciate every small kindness and to brush off slights that would once have wounded him deeply.

Through it all, he never lost the fundamental hope that had led him to Mumbai. At times, he would pause on the sidewalk, watching city buses roar by, jam-packed with office workers, students, and hawkers. He wondered if any of them had started out as he had, homeless and desperate. He recalled his mother's eye medicine business in the village and how resourcefulness had helped his family survive back home. Perhaps there was a parallel in Mumbai. Perhaps if he remained open to new ideas and persisted, he, too, could climb out of these circumstances.

Meanwhile, Mama's skill as a cobbler occasionally came in handy. Some residents of the area asked him to patch up their chappals or mend small leather items. It was not a big source of income, but it reminded Mama of his roots. Polishing and repairing shoes was something he understood, something he could do well if given the chance. Over time, he toyed with the idea of setting up a small repair station in a busy area—maybe near a train station or a market. Yet, that dream required a little capital to buy tools and rent a patch of pavement. For now, all he could do was keep the idea in mind, saving whatever small amounts he could.

As the 1950s advanced, Mumbai grew faster still, and more rural migrants poured into the city in search of work. Tensions sometimes flared between established residents and newcomers competing for the same limited jobs. Mama, however, kept mostly to himself. His world revolved around the daily schedule: wake up at the flower stall, polish shoes near Crawford Market, wander to Zaveri Bazaar, possibly return to the wholesale market in the late afternoon, and then back to Kala Chowki by nightfall. Every so often, he tried something new—like visiting the docks to see if any cargo ships were hiring casual labor—but success did not come easily.

Yet, this routine, though exhausting, served a purpose: it built Mama's perseverance. Each day he walked the city streets, forging a mental map of where certain businesses clustered, which neighborhoods might have wealthier customers, and how best to approach potential clients. He picked up bits of Hindi along with his Marathi, enough to speak to traders from northern India who had also settled in Mumbai. On slow days, when few people wanted their shoes polished, he would linger near the flower stall, listening to passing conversations for any mention of job openings. If he overheard someone say that a certain factory was hiring or that a nearby building needed a watchman, Mama would note it mentally and investigate the next day.

Throughout these trials, he maintained a consistent refrain in his mind: "This is not permanent. I will find a way." The city's sheer scale hinted that new doors could open unexpectedly if he persevered. Meanwhile, the memory of village life—its crippling poverty and limited education—reminded him that going back prematurely would simply lead him back to the same barriers. Even on nights when the rumble of vehicles or the patter of monsoon rain prevented him from sleeping, he consoled himself that the city, for all its difficulties, offered more hope than hopelessness.

Mama's days on the streets of Mumbai were fraught with danger, disappointment, and discomfort, yet they also honed an unbreakable spirit. This chapter—his first steps into the metropolis—represents a turning point in his life's journey. Despite lacking formal guidance or institutional support, he utilized every asset he had: the initiative to approach potential customers, the humility to accept help from a flower seller, and the willingness to adapt to changing circumstances.

In many ways, these were the earliest tests of the leadership qualities that would later define him. The harshness of slum living gave him compassion for those who struggled in overlooked corners of society. Polishing shoes in busy markets introduced him to a cross-section of people, expanding his understanding of commerce, aspiration, and everyday survival in the city. His persistent attempts at finding stable work, no matter how small the job, demonstrated a work ethic built on patience and tenacity.

Looking back, one might see a direct link from these months of itinerant labor to the empathy and resolve that would later fuel Mama's political and social endeavors. He had been down at the lowest rung of the urban hierarchy, vying for coins on the street, and yet never lost the sense that the future could hold more. Although immediate prospects seemed bleak, seeds of ambition continued to sprout, strengthened by each incremental success—a single good day of polishing shoes, a helpful exchange with a potential employer, or a few extra coins saved from a small repair job.

Mama's first years in Mumbai stand out as a poignant illustration of hope meeting reality. Drawn by the possibility of earning an income that might uplift his family, he arrived in the city only to discover that navigating the slums and street life required every ounce of resourcefulness he possessed. From sleeping at Bus Stop No. 44 in Kala Chowki to forging a friendship with a benevolent flower seller, Mama's survival hinged on building connections in unexpected places.

At the heart of it all was a determination that refused to be smothered by the city's chaos. He refused to let meager wages or cramped living spaces break his spirit. Instead, he saw each challenge as part of a larger odyssey—one that might eventually lead him to stable ground. In a harsh metropolis, he clung to small acts of kindness, like being allowed to store his bedding at the flower stall, which reminded him that people, no matter how burdened by their own struggles, could still look out for each other.

Though life in the slum and on the streets was far from the promise of a thriving career, it gave Mama a taste of Mumbai's complexity. He glimpsed the ruthless competition for menial jobs, the spark of big-city dreams in the eyes of countless migrants, and the resilience required to persist day after day. Above all, this period underscored that every small opportunity—a single shoe polish, a minor repair job—could serve as a building block toward something greater.

CHAPTER SIX

Early Years of Survival in the City

For a young Sitaram "Mama" Ghandat, the first few years in Mumbai tested every ounce of will he possessed. Though he had arrived with high hopes reality set in as he discovered just how difficult it was to secure stable employment in a vast and competitive city. Over a period of two to two-and-a-half years, Mama's daily routine centered on finding enough work to cover a modest meal and a safe (or at least tolerated) corner to sleep. In a place teeming with newcomers who had equally urgent needs, his struggle to earn a foothold was marked by long days, minimal income, and resilience that grew out of necessity.

This chapter delves into that early phase of Mama's journey in Mumbai: the unpredictable hustle, the relationships he built with local traders, his trials in shoe polishing for gold shop owners, and the small beacon of hope he found in securing an employment card. By exploring this chapter in detail, we gain insight into how these years solidified Mama's tenacity and revealed the opportunities for growth hidden even in the harshest circumstances.

After arriving in Mumbai, Mama quickly realized that the city, despite its promise of better prospects, offered no immediate or guaranteed route to financial security. Large sections of the population already worked in mills, ports, or small shops, and many of these workplaces did not actively seek new hires unless they had specific skills or strong references. Standing in job queues outside textile mills and factories often proved fruitless, as security guards turned away newcomers without formal papers or experience. Mama, with no more than a 4th-standard education, lacked both a specialized craft and social connections in the city, making him just one of the thousands struggling in the informal job market.

During these first 2–2.5 years, daily survival consumed most of Mama's energy. Waking up before dawn—often at Bus Stop No. 44 in Kala Chowki, where he initially slept—he would gather his few belongings and set out on foot. On good days, he would trek to areas like Crawford Market or Zaveri Bazaar before the crowds arrived, hoping to catch early business in shoe polishing or odd tasks. On less hopeful days, he might simply roam the city's backstreets, introducing himself to vendors or shop owners, asking if they needed an extra hand. Sometimes he helped unload crates from delivery trucks for a pittance; other times, he approached small eateries, offering to clean tables or wash dishes. Although these short-term gigs helped him scrounge for daily meals, none turned into the stable job he desired.

The city's rhythm, marked by relentless movement and competition, underscored Mama's predicament. He watched other laborers dash from one part of town to another, chasing rumors of better wages or more substantial contracts. He noticed how men with specialized skills—tailors, machinists, electricians—could sometimes command higher pay, even if they came from humble backgrounds. Meanwhile, Mama, with limited training beyond the basics of cobbler work, had to rely on his wits and stamina to secure day-to-day survival. This period of uncertainty taught him humility: in a city filled with millions of stories, his was just one more tale of a newcomer trying to climb the ladder.

Meanwhile, Mama's own siblings were forging varied paths. Growing up in the same rural village, each brother had chosen a different route to combat poverty. One had found employment in a mill. The mill job was physically demanding—long hours spent operating machines in dimly lit, dusty hall halls—but it provided a somewhat predictable wage, even if it was minimal. This brother made do with cramped mill quarters or tiny rented rooms shared with fellow workers, counting on each monthly paycheck to cover basic necessities.

Another brother remained in the village, continuing the family's cobbler trade in a more traditional sense. While Mama and the other siblings had ventured to the city, this brother opted to stay close to their parents, occasionally visiting neighboring villages to repair shoes or sandals. Though the rural economy was far from lucrative, he preferred the stability of known surroundings to the chaos of the metropolis. The daily routine there, at least, involved fewer surprises and the comfort of a small but loyal customer base.

In contrast, Mama's own journey seemed more uncertain. As he spent his days moving between Crawford Market, Zaveri Bazaar, and other pockets of Mumbai, he saw the benefits his brothers had in their respective paths—regular mill wages or the familiarity of rural life—yet he was determined to prove that the city could yield better possibilities if one was willing to endure hardship. He did feel pangs of doubt. On especially tough days, with barely enough money for food, he wondered if returning to the village might be wiser. But the flicker of hope that had first drawn him to Mumbai remained unextinguished. If others could navigate the city's complexities, he believed, so could he.

This divergence among the siblings revealed how the same family background could lead to vastly different experiences. None of them had it easy—each faced a version of poverty, limited schooling, and the burden of supporting parents back home. Yet Mama's choice to remain in Mumbai reflected a distinct sense of ambition. He refused to settle for a situation he deemed unsatisfactory, even if that meant years of scraping by on the streets.

Amid these struggles, one figure stood out as a modest guide in Mama's life: Devaram Gaikwad. He was not a wealthy patron or a relative with endless resources; rather, he was someone who recognized Mama's desperation and offered a simple piece of advice that could have far-reaching consequences. Devaram explained that the government maintained a registration system for casual laborers and job seekers—an "employment card" that people could apply for and renew annually. In a city like Mumbai, where competition for every job was fierce, having one's name on an official list might open doors that would otherwise remain closed.

Mama latched onto this idea, seeing it as a rare signpost in his otherwise directionless search for work. Early one morning, he set aside his usual routine of heading straight to the markets and made his way to the appropriate government office. The line was long, filled with weary men clutching tattered documents, each hoping for a chance at better employment. When Mama finally reached the counter, he presented the few papers he had—a basic identity document, perhaps a letter of reference from someone in the city, or details from his village. The clerk filled out forms, asked cursory questions about Mama's background, and, after taking a small fee, handed him an official employment card.

The card itself did not guarantee a job. But it symbolized a step toward legitimacy in a place where Mama had felt invisible. Now, if a government or semi-government position for a peon, messenger, or low-level staffer opened up, Mama's name might surface in a database of registered applicants. He was also instructed to renew the card every year, keeping his information up to date. Though this meant another recurring expense and time spent waiting in bureaucratic queues, Mama saw it as a minor inconvenience in exchange for a possible foothold in more stable work.

Renewing the card became part of his annual routine. He might have been sleeping behind a flower stall or on a bus stop bench, but once a year, he presented himself at the government office in clean clothes, carefully borrowed or saved for just such an occasion. Each renewal felt like a small affirmation that he was still in the running, still determined to find a job that paid a consistent wage. In the labyrinth of the city's underemployment and informal hustle, this piece of paper felt like a lifeline.

Despite taking this constructive step, Mama's day-to-day life remained precarious. Balancing his shoe-polishing work across the city left him physically exhausted. After trekking from one location to another, he often arrived at the flower stall late at night, too tired to do more than unroll his bedding and fall asleep. Meals were sporadic; some days he could afford a modest plate of dal and rice, while on others he subsisted on the cheapest snacks available. The scorching summers brought heat that made standing on the roadsides nearly unbearable, and the monsoon rains threatened to soak his meager belongings, rendering them useless or prone to mildew.

He also encountered petty theft and occasional altercations on the streets. The sidewalk economy attracted not only people seeking honest living but also those preying on vulnerable newcomers. More than once, Mama found himself jostled or forced to pay a small "fee" to someone claiming to control a particular patch of pavement for shoe polishing. Survival required constant vigilance, especially for a man carrying the few coins he earned each day.

Yet, amid all of this, Mama retained a sense of purpose. Unlike some disillusioned youths who gave in to anger or resignation, Mama quietly reminded himself why he had come to Mumbai in the first place: to improve his lot and, if possible, send some help back home. Though he had little to show for his efforts in the immediate sense—no real room or consistent job—he refused to accept that this was all fate had in store.

In many ways, these early years were an education more profound than any structured syllabus. Mama learned how traders operated, how supply chains fed neighborhoods, and how even small tasks could be monetized. He saw how quickly word of mouth spread about a reliable service—if his shoe polishing was efficient and courteous, he might gain two or three repeat customers who would then tell their colleagues. The city, for all its impersonality, could reward diligence in unexpected ways.

He also discovered the importance of alliances and friendships, no matter how informal. At Crawford Market, the goodwill of a single merchant might shield him from a competitor's jealousy or provide him a little corner to stash his tools. At Zaveri Bazaar, a gold shop guard who became familiar with Mama might wave him through without suspicion. And at the flower stall near Kala Chowki, he found a secure spot for his bedding each night, courtesy of a kindly vendor who had once been a newcomer himself.

These small networks underscored a significant truth: no one made it in the city alone. Whether rich or poor, everyone depended on various relationships—formal, informal, fleeting, or enduring—to navigate the urban sprawl. Though Mama lacked the typical resources of an established migrant—such as family members who could offer lodging or job referrals—he compensated by forging trust wherever he could. His willingness to work hard, accept small payments graciously, and remain respectful, even in the face of insults, set him apart from those who grew resentful or impatient.

Over the course of these 2–2.5 years, a subtle but real shift began to take place in Mama's life. While still far from comfortable, he accumulated a bit more knowledge and a slightly broader support network. Now, if a certain lane in Zaveri Bazaar proved too competitive one day, he knew to head early to Crawford Market instead, or vice versa. He had the confidence to strike up conversations with new traders, introducing himself as someone who could handle shoe repairs or polishing quickly. And with each annual renewal of his employment card, he felt a faint but growing sense of belonging in the city's administrative machinery.

By the time he neared the end of this phase, Mama recognized that he had at least two potential paths. One was to continue in the informal sector, gradually trying to expand his shoe-related business or secure a small corner stall where he could work. The other was to hold out for a more permanent job, possibly through the government channels made accessible by his employment card. He did not know which path would bear fruit first, but he trusted that his persistent effort would eventually yield an opening.

To a casual observer, Mama's situation might have looked static—still no permanent lodging, no steady salary, and no major breakthrough. But inside, he was changing. His street sense sharpened, his humility deepened, and his resilience developed layer by layer. Days of hunger alternated with days when a surprise windfall made him believe wholeheartedly that tomorrow could be better than today. Each small triumph—like a customer returning for a second polishing or a trader remembering his name—reinforced his resolve to keep going.

Although no single achievement marked the close of these early survival years, Mama did move forward, inch by inch, from the precarious edge of homelessness toward a lifestyle that, while still minimal, allowed him to envision a future in the city. The guidance from Devaram Gaikwad regarding the employment card shone like a small lantern in the dark, showing that more structured job opportunities might eventually surface. Meanwhile, Mama's day-to-day hustle taught him to be flexible, to keep his eyes open for the next lead, and to value even the smallest successes in a place where tens of thousands struggled just like him.

What these 2–2.5 years formed, more than anything, was the backbone of resilience that would serve Mama well in the challenges yet to come. From sleeping behind the flower stall at night to bargaining with gold shop owners for a chance to polish their shoes, he stretched every possibility to survive and, more importantly, to remain hopeful. The city tested him, toughened him, and—slowly but surely—prepared him for roles in life that would require not just hard work, but also insight into the lives of those struggling at the bottom of the urban hierarchy.

As we close this chapter, it's important to recognize that Mama's journey in these years was about more than just scrounging for coins. It was about discovering who he could be under pressure, forging bonds in unexpected places, and maintaining a sense of personal worth even when the world around him seemed to offer no validation. Through it all, Mama stayed committed to his vision of forging a better life—one day at a time, one polished shoe at a time, and one renewed employment card at a time.

CHAPTER SEVEN

MARRIAGE AND NEW RESPONSIBILITIES

The moment of marriage is a pivotal one in any life, but for Sitaram "Mama" Ghandat, this milestone carried particular weight. After years of scraping by in Mumbai—polishing shoes, searching for regular work, and sleeping wherever he could—he was about to step into a new realm of personal responsibility. Marriage brought not only companionship but also the realities of starting a household on a meager income, balancing work obligations with family duties, and grappling with the ever-present financial struggles he had known all his life. In this chapter, we see how Mama's marriage was arranged in a modest chawl community, the humble wedding ceremony itself, and the challenges he faced trying to ensure that his new wife and future children could thrive despite limited resources.

Mama had been living in Mumbai for a while, finding various ways to survive. Although he did not earn much, he gradually became known within the local chawl (tenement) community as a patient, diligent, and caring individual. Many people in his neighborhood appreciated that he worked hard polishing shoes, doing minor cobbler repairs, and taking on side tasks. Over time, some noticed his sympathetic nature—he would help neighbors carry groceries up steep staircases, or he might fetch water when an older neighbor was too weak to stand in the queue at the communal tap. Such small deeds added up, and the community respected him.

In those years, marriages within chawls often occurred through personal connections rather than formal matchmaking services. Parents, relatives, or older residents of the neighborhood would spot a potential alliance and make introductions. The thought process was simple: if a young man seemed upright, steady, and responsible—no matter how modest his income—he could be considered a decent candidate for marriage. This was especially so in communities where everyone shared the same general hardships, so expectations were realistic.

Eventually, Mama's father, who still had a say in his son's future, encouraged him to marry. Since Mama no longer lived in the village, the search for a suitable bride took place mostly in the city, guided by mutual acquaintances and extended relatives who had migrated to similar chawls. The bride-to-be lived in the same compound where Mama stayed or visited daily. She had a reputation for being helpful to her own family, resourceful in household tasks, and accepting of life's challenges—qualities that resonated with Mama's own experiences.

Though Mama himself might have met her in passing—perhaps near a shared water tap or while climbing the crowded stairwells—the formal arrangement required both families to give their approval. At that time, it was common for prospective brides and grooms to see each other once or twice, often with a chaperone present, before the marriage was finalized. According to relatives, the meeting was brief and straightforward: they exchanged a few shy words, saw that they came from similar backgrounds, and left the final decision to their parents. Within a short span, all parties gave a nod of agreement. The match was set.

Weddings in financially constrained communities typically lacked the grandeur one might see in upscale city ceremonies. Instead, they focused on the essential elements: a ritual to solemnize the union, the presence of family and neighbors, and a simple meal to celebrate. In Mama's case, the ceremony occurred in an open space within the chawl itself—an area that might otherwise be used for children to play or for neighbors to gather laundry. He could not afford a lavish hall or a decorated pavilion, so he and his family improvised with whatever resources were at hand.

Friends and relatives borrowed a few thin sarees to use as a makeshift canopy, tying them across bamboo poles or wooden supports to create a semblance of a mandap. This colorful but humble arrangement signaled that a wedding was taking place, even though the materials and decorations were minimal. Onlookers saw the fluttering sarees in the afternoon breeze and understood that a new chapter was about to begin for Mama and his bride.

The bride's family contributed what they could—a few traditional items like turmeric and kumkum for the rituals, possibly some borrowed jewelry for the bride to wear, and small gifts for Mama's relatives. Mama's side pooled modest amounts of money to arrange a simple spread of food. Neighbors chipped in too, providing extra utensils, open stoves, or assistance in cooking large pots of rice and dal. While it was not a feast by any measure, it carried the warmth of collective goodwill. People who had shared hardships for years were excited to see a moment of joy and new beginnings.

On the day of the wedding, Mama, dressed in a freshly washed shirt and simple trousers (or perhaps a borrowed suit jacket if someone could spare one), stood beneath the saree canopy, waiting for his bride to join him. A small crowd of friends, extended family, and curious neighbors gathered around. Children peeked from balconies above, giggling at the sight. The officiant or local priest performed the essential rituals—tying the sacred thread, applying auspicious marks on their foreheads, and having them exchange garlands. A few women in the community might have broken into spontaneous songs, adding a traditional flavor to an otherwise minimalistic ceremony. The entire event lasted only a few hours, culminating in blessings from elders who wished the couple a stable and healthy partnership.

To an outsider, the wedding might have seemed exceedingly modest, but for Mama and his bride, the thin sarees and borrowed cooking pots held immense symbolic power. They had each other, the support of the chawl, and the determination to forge a life together despite the constraints. In their eyes, the ceremony's simplicity was not a marker of deprivation but a testament to shared effort, unity, and the hope that things would improve.

Following the wedding, Mama and his wife needed a space of their own. Though his own living conditions had been unstable—sometimes sleeping behind a flower stall or at a bus stop—marriage changed the equation. He felt a responsibility to provide a semblance of privacy and comfort, however rudimentary. The newlyweds soon found a small room in the same chawl where they had gotten married, likely with a single window or a tiny ventilation space, and a shared bathroom somewhere at the end of the corridor.

Rent was modest by city standards, but it still posed a challenge given Mama's unpredictable income. The landlord, a chawl owner or caretaker, might have been lenient on some occasions but insisted on punctual payment once the month ended. The room was too small to separate into distinct living and sleeping areas, so the couple arranged their few belongings against the walls, creating a patch of floor space for a simple bedroll at night. Boxes or trunks, if they could afford them, stored clothing and essential utensils. Sometimes, a single light bulb hanging from the ceiling served as both the kitchen lamp and living room illumination.

Despite its cramped nature, this tiny room represented progress. Mama's wife contributed to the household by managing daily chores—filling water buckets early in the morning, preparing basic meals like roti and sabzi, and tidying up the limited space. Meanwhile, Mama continued his cobbler work, setting up a small corner in front of the chawl if possible or taking his tools to busier commercial areas during the day. He would spend long hours trying to attract customers, hoping to polish or repair enough shoes to meet the rent and buy groceries. Their meal plan typically revolved around cheap staples like rice, dal, or simple vegetables, with special treats reserved for rare occasions.

The hustle and bustle of chawl life had its advantages. Neighbors were close at hand, and although privacy was minimal, mutual assistance was often part of the culture. If Mama's wife ran out of cooking oil, she could borrow a bit from the woman next door until payday. In return, she might share leftover chapatis or keep an eye on the neighbor's children while the neighbor ran errands. This informal support network helped them navigate the daily grind without feeling entirely isolated.

Mama's new responsibilities meant balancing his role as a husband—and, later, as a father—with the demands of scraping together a livelihood. Prior to marriage, he could sleep wherever he found space, skip meals to save money, and pivot his schedule without consulting anyone. Now, he had another person relying on him for basic shelter and sustenance. The emotional weight of that obligation was both motivating and stressful.

On a typical day, Mama would rise before dawn, perhaps sipping a cup of hot tea if they could afford milk and tea leaves. Then he would gather his cobbler's box—containing brushes, polishes, spare leather patches, needles, and threads—and walk toward his usual haunts. Sometimes he set up near a bus stop where office-goers might pass by, or by the local market where vendors needed sturdy footwear to endure the muddy or dusty conditions. In the afternoon, the scorching sun might force him to take a short break, returning to the chawl for a drink of water and a quick meal if his wife had prepared one. Then, in the late afternoon or early evening, he might venture out again, hoping for a last wave of customers heading home from work.

If business was decent that day, Mama would return to the chawl with a small sum in hand—enough to purchase lentils, vegetables, and maybe some small treat. His wife, meanwhile, stayed engaged in the never-ending tasks of housekeeping in a chawl setting. Together, they would share dinner on a low stool or mat, discussing the day's events and strategizing how to meet upcoming expenses. Rent, water bills, small medical needs, or occasional new clothes all demanded careful budgeting.

On the many days when business was slow, the pressures mounted. Mama might return home almost empty-handed, feeling guilt and anxiety gnawing at him. In such moments, he would sometimes recall the advice of older chawl residents who said, "Work comes in waves. Keep your tools ready, treat your customers kindly, and tomorrow might be better." Mama learned to cling to these words, drawing on the same perseverance that had kept him afloat before marriage. Now, however, his motivation took on a different angle: it was not only about his survival but also about ensuring that his new family did not go hungry or lose the roof over their heads.

When earnings were insufficient, Mama occasionally turned to borrowing as a temporary solution. A surprising source of such financial help, though not ideal, came from the local liquor store in Ambewadi (the neighborhood area around Kala Chowki). This was not a conventional bank or credit society—just a local shop where people might buy small amounts of liquor in the evenings or weekends. The shop owner, who knew Mama and recognized his sincerity, offered short-term loans on days when Mama fell behind.

Borrowing from a liquor store was not an uncommon practice in some chawl communities, simply because formal avenues for credit—such as banks or regulated loan services—were beyond reach for families with no stable employment or collateral. Interest rates on these informal loans could be higher than standard rates, but the arrangement was flexible and based on personal trust. The store owner would note in a small notebook how much Mama had borrowed, expecting repayment within a short time.

Mama was acutely aware of the risks. Failing to repay could strain the relationship and ruin his standing in the neighborhood. Moreover, repeated loans could trap him in a cycle of debt if not managed carefully. Yet, on those particular days when there was literally no money to buy groceries, borrowing became the only way to feed his wife or pay the chawl rent to avoid eviction. From Mama's perspective, ensuring basic sustenance and a stable shelter overshadowed the embarrassment or fear tied to these small debts.

At the start of each new month, the couple scrambled to repay as many outstanding bits of debt as possible, using whatever Mama earned from the shoe repairs or other odd jobs he might land. This constant juggling of daily income and personal loans added tension to their household, but they approached it as a team, discussing priorities and deciding which bills to pay first.

These newly married years, though rife with financial stress, also transformed Mama on a personal level. Where he had once roamed the streets alone, guided primarily by his own immediate needs, he now carried the weight of someone else's well-being on his shoulders. This shift brought moments of pride—like when he managed to bring home groceries without borrowing money—or evenings when his wife thanked him for the day's efforts with a hot meal and a kind word. In these small victories, Mama found a sense of purpose he had not fully experienced before.

Community elders noticed the changes in Mama's demeanor. He spoke less of returning to the village or searching for entirely new ventures; instead, he channeled his energy into perfecting his cobbler skills or scouting better locations to ply his trade. Occasionally, an older neighbor might offer him advice on managing household finances: "Buy staples in bulk at the start of the month—dal, wheat, flour—so you don't pay higher prices in small quantities." Even though Mama's earnings were modest, such tips sometimes helped stretch the budget a little further.

At the same time, the weight of responsibility could be isolating. Friends or relatives who lived in the same chawl might invite him to small gatherings or social events, but Mama often had to decline, worried about spending money or leaving his wife alone in their cramped room. Some nights he lay awake, mentally tallying how many shoe repairs he needed to perform the next day just to meet upcoming expenses. If the monsoon rains arrived early, flooding the streets and scaring away customers, it could upend his fragile plans in an instant.

Yet, Mama chose not to let these setbacks define him. Much like in his earlier days, when he navigated street life with relentless determination, he approached marital and financial obstacles as challenges to be overcome step by step. The presence of a supportive wife, even if she sometimes grew anxious, provided emotional ballast. She believed in his grit, reminding him that every household in the chawl struggled with similar problems. While this reminder did not erase the bills, it at least underscored that they were not alone in their fight.

Despite the ongoing trials, the young couple's life was not devoid of joys. A rare day of better business—when more customers needed shoe repairs—might mean they could afford a slightly more elaborate meal: perhaps a vegetable curry instead of just dal, or a small piece of fish if the market price was right. If Mama happened to receive a small tip from a satisfied customer, he might indulge in a sweet treat for his wife, recalling how he once, as a child, stole a single coin from his mother to buy himself a treat. Now, his small acts of generosity were tied to the family unit he was building.

Sometimes, neighbors would invite them to simple birthday gatherings or religious festivities, where everyone contributed a little food. Such occasions allowed Mama and his wife to momentarily forget their financial anxieties, sharing laughter and conversation under the dim bulbs of the chawl corridors. These nights reminded them that life in a cramped community was not all hardship. Tight bonds and collective compassion often flourished where resources were scarce.

There were also tender moments that underscored how marriage had deepened Mama's empathy. If he arrived home with barely any earnings, his wife comforted him, assuring him that they would manage with a thin dal and leftover chapatis until the next day. If, on the other hand, she felt overwhelmed by house chores or the relentless beep of the neighbors' radios echoing through thin walls, Mama offered to help with cooking or water-fetching before he returned to polishing shoes. Though small in scale, such gestures strengthened their bond, affirming that they were partners confronting a difficult environment together.

Looking back, the early phase of Mama's marriage and new responsibilities offers valuable insights into how a person grows under pressure. While his earlier life had revolved around personal survival—finding a meal, a safe sleeping spot, or any small source of income—now he had to think in terms of household stability. The thin sarees in the wedding mandap symbolized the fragility of this new beginning, while the cramped chawl room reminded him daily that resourcefulness was essential for managing rent and bills.

During these years, Mama gained invaluable life lessons that shaped his approach to financial stability, relationships, and community engagement. Budgeting and debt management became a crucial skill as he struggled to balance irregular earnings with predictable expenses like rent. He discovered that trust-based loans, even from unexpected sources like a liquor store, could provide short-term relief but also posed the risk of falling into a cycle of debt. Breaking free from this pattern required immense discipline and careful planning.

Marriage brought a new perspective on financial responsibility, transforming decision-making from an individual effort into a shared burden. Every financial shortfall and borrowed coin became a mutual concern, and Mama's wife played a significant role by offering both moral support and practical labor. Their partnership strengthened his resilience, teaching him the importance of collaboration in overcoming hardships.

The chawl, despite its noise and lack of privacy, provided a crucial communal safety net. Neighbors who recognized Mama's sincerity extended support in various ways—offering advice, moral encouragement, and occasional short-term assistance. This sense of community reinforced the idea that social ties could act as an informal yet powerful financial buffer during difficult times.

Emotionally, the stakes were higher now that he had a household to support. The early frustrations of empty earnings and threats of eviction tested his endurance, but they also shaped an unshakable determination. These trials fortified his resolve and prepared him for the larger challenges he would face in the future.

Ultimately, these experiences laid the foundation for his approach to leadership, both in his professional and community roles. A man who had once juggled small coins to pay rent could empathize deeply with others navigating similar struggles, making him a more compassionate and grounded leader.

Mama's marriage marked a subtle turning point in his life's trajectory. Gone were the days when he could simply adapt to his own solitary needs. Now, with a wife relying on his income and moral support, he had to escalate his efforts in polishing shoes, repairing sandals, and searching for any odd job that might augment his daily earnings. The simple wedding mandap—merely a few thin sarees draped in a narrow chawl courtyard—captured both the limitations and aspirations that defined this new phase. Even though money was tight, the sense of unity and shared purpose shone through every borrowed pot, every neighborly favor, and every creative solution to daily survival.

In the cramped home they rented, Mama discovered the power of small joys: a pot of freshly made dal, an appreciative neighbor's smile, or a brief moment of rest after a long day's work. Inevitably, there were setbacks, sometimes leading him to borrow from places like the local liquor store—a stark reminder that for those living on the margins, any small crisis could spiral into deeper debt. Yet, neither Mama nor his wife let these difficulties extinguish the spirit of their union. Instead, they learned to navigate life with the unwavering belief that tomorrow could bring more customers, a kinder landlord, or simply an extra bit of hope.

These early marital years not only shaped Mama's character but also influenced how he would later approach broader social and personal endeavors. In a city where so many were caught in the grind of low-wage work and precarious housing, Mama's experiences mirrored the realities of countless others. He belonged to a larger narrative of survival and perseverance that defined communities living in the shadow of towering skyscrapers. And like many who quietly endured, he found that responsibility—when coupled with a patient, steady determination—could become a catalyst for growth. Each day was another chance to provide for his new family, to honor the vows exchanged beneath those thin sarees, and to carve out a life, however humble, in the vastness of Mumbai.

Though the financial burdens and everyday struggles were far from resolved at this point, one crucial certainty emerged: marriage gave Mama a tangible reason to keep striving. His wife's presence made the chawl feel like a home rather than just a temporary shelter. Their shared resilience fostered a sense of purpose that propelled Mama onward, even through the harshest setbacks.

CHAPTER EIGHT

THE POST OFFICE

By the time Sitaram "Mama" Ghandat received a call to join the Fort Post Office, he had already endured many trials in Mumbai. From polishing shoes at street corners and sleeping on bus stops to juggling marriage and chawl life on a meager income, he navigated a city that rarely gave second chances. Yet the faint promise of stable employment—especially in a government setting—was too significant to ignore. All those annual renewals of his employment card, standing in winding queues and handing over modest fees, had finally borne fruit.

Each year, Mama dutifully renewed his employment card, a registration document meant to help people without specialized credentials find government or semi-government positions. He had discovered this system through an acquaintance, Devaram Gaikwad, who urged him to keep his name on the rolls. Though the repeated trips to a cramped municipal office felt tedious, Mama saw it as a thin but vital line connecting him to potential opportunities beyond daily cobbler work.

Finally, a letter or notification arrived at his chawl address—likely on a day when Mama was out polishing shoes. His wife, used to receiving mostly bills or the occasional family note, was astonished to see an official envelope. Inside, a short directive asked Mama to report for an aptitude test at the Fort Post Office. The position in question: a mail-delivery role that required bicycling routes and sorting letters. Even though Mama had only basic literacy in Marathi (and barely any in English), the prospect of a stable paycheck and possible government benefits was exhilarating. His immediate thought was: "At last, something might change for the better."

He recalled how, in his younger days, he had spotted postmen weaving through narrow lanes on bicycles, delivering letters and packages. Their uniforms carried an air of respect; people often opened doors with a friendly "Namaste" for the postman because he was the bearer of news—good or bad. The idea of stepping into that role felt surreal to Mama. Could he, with a 4th-standard education, manage official duties on behalf of the Indian postal system? All he knew was that he wouldn't squander a chance that had taken so long to appear.

Upon arriving at the Fort Post Office—a grand colonial building with towering arches and hectic lines of customers—Mama was directed to a courtyard area. Here, a small cluster of applicants were waiting, each carrying identity proofs and essential papers. Some wore neat shirts, while others had the look of day laborers hoping for a break. An official explained the rules: to qualify for the mail-delivery role, each candidate had to ride a bicycle in a figure-8 pattern without losing balance or stepping foot on the ground. The post office, it turned out, valued this skill because postmen frequently needed to navigate tight lanes and corners in busy areas.

Mama had ridden a bicycle before, but only in the most basic sense—short distances, straight lines, perhaps around the quieter edges of the city or the outskirts of his village. He had never tried a controlled figure-8 track under watchful eyes. The official demonstration showed a white-powder outline on the ground, shaped like two loops joined in the middle. Each rider had to follow the track precisely, a test of balance and control. A single wobble outside the chalk lines would mean failing.

When it was Mama's turn, his nerves flared. He could feel beads of sweat forming on his forehead, partly from the mid-day heat, partly from the realization that this small test could determine the rest of his life. Taking a deep breath, he mounted the bicycle and pedalled forward. The first loop felt manageable, and as he approached the central intersection—where the figure-8 curves sharply—he focused on keeping steady. With careful balance and controlled movements, he managed to complete the pattern without error. A moment of silence followed before the observer gave a brief nod of approval.

Relief flooded Mama's chest as he stepped off the bicycle. He had passed the test on his first attempt, securing his place in the next stage of the selection process. Though the challenge had been intimidating, his ability to remain composed under pressure proved invaluable. This moment reinforced his belief that preparation and focus could overcome even the most unexpected hurdles.

Though the biggest worry—the figure-8—was resolved, Mama sensed an even larger challenge looming: the issue of reading addresses, many of which were written in English. During a brief chat with the recruiter, Mama learned that the job required not just physical delivery but also the sorting of letters by street names, building numbers, and occasionally entire addresses typed out in English script. The official explained that postmen typically had to verify addresses, match them to official listings, and sometimes fill out receipts or signature logs, also in English.

Mama's own literacy skills were limited to Marathi, and his English reading was close to nonexistent. He recognized basic letters—an A, a B, maybe a few others—but reading entire words or comprehending addresses was a monumental leap. Nevertheless, he tried to maintain composure, telling himself that maybe he could learn on the job. After all, he had learned to ride a figure-8 bicycle track in a week; perhaps with enough dedication, English addresses wouldn't be an impossible barrier.

Once formally accepted, Mama donned a simple uniform—likely a khaki shirt and trousers—that labeled him as a postal employee. He reported to the Fort Post Office early each morning, where a supervisor showed him how letters and parcels were organized. Rows of pigeonhole shelves, each labeled with location codes or route names, lined a large sorting hall. Experienced postmen swiftly distributed mail into appropriate slots, scanning addresses with practiced speed. In the corner, new hires like Mama tried to emulate them, albeit clumsily.

During those first few days, Mama's anxiety skyrocketed. He watched others read "Marine Drive," "Chowpatty," or "Ballard Estate" addresses in a blink, sometimes even deciphering partially smudged text. By contrast, Mama felt lost. If an address was in Marathi, he stood a chance, but any English text beyond the simplest brand names or place names was baffling. He also discovered that some letters carried instructions or official stamps in English that he couldn't decode.

At times, a kind colleague would spot Mama's struggle and offer a quick explanation: "Here, that spells 'Colaba.' This is an address near Regal Circle." He would nod appreciatively, but the next day brought a fresh wave of unfamiliar words. Worse yet, Mama feared making mistakes. Misdelivering mail could cost someone a vital letter—an exam result, a legal notice, or a job offer. The pressure weighed heavily on him. He worried that any day now, a supervisor might scold him or even terminate him for incompetence.

And it wasn't just about the job: Mama's wife, relatives, and neighbors in the chawl had begun to express excitement. A government post was considered respectable, a chance for stable pay and potential career growth. The news had likely reached Mama's parents in the village, who saw it as a dream come true: their son, once relegated to poverty, was now an official postman in Mumbai. With each passing day, the gap between outward expectations and Mama's inner turmoil grew sharper.

Desperate to improve, Mama tried to memorize common English words used in addresses. After finishing each day's shift, he might slip a few old envelopes into his pocket—discarded or sample ones—and take them home. At night, in the dim glow of a single bulb, he traced the letters, comparing them to Marathi scripts in an attempt to form mental links. Sometimes he sat with a battered English-Marathi dictionary borrowed from a neighbor, painstakingly matching words to possible pronunciations.

Despite these efforts, progress was slow. English addresses often included abbreviations—St. for Street, Rd. for Road, Bldg. for Building—that baffled Mama. On top of that, the city was filled with place names derived from diverse languages—Khar, Bandra, Masjid Bunder, Lalbaug—and not all addresses adhered to a standard format. The unspoken assumption was that a postman should already be well-versed in reading them.

The more Mama tried, the more exhausted he became. His wife did her best to encourage him—cooking simple dinners, urging him to rest—but every day brought new mistakes. It didn't help that Mama's supervisor sometimes rushed the training process, expecting him to sort a certain number of letters daily. If Mama lagged, the supervisor would throw him a disapproving glance. Even some colleagues began to see him as a liability; a misfiled letter in the sorting racks could wreak havoc on an entire shift.

Occasionally, Mama considered talking to a manager about his literacy issues, but shame and fear held him back. He worried they'd revoke his appointment on the spot. In fleeting moments, he thought of how he had surmounted the figure-8 challenge by practicing late into the night. Perhaps, if he just worked harder at reading, he could eventually cope. Yet the backlog of unknown words piled up faster than his learning curve.

Despite Mama's determination, the mental strain reached a critical level. Each morning, as he donned his khaki uniform, dread gnawed at him. He was expected to deliver mail across busy neighborhoods, cross-referencing English addresses with route maps that also used English labels. A single route might have dozens of letters, each demanding that the postman locate the correct building or door. The job required not just literacy but also street-level knowledge that took weeks—if not months—to develop.

Mama found himself making small errors. Supervisors scolded him for slow performance, and recipients complained if mail arrived late. Some residents, especially those used to quick postal service, grew impatient seeing a confused postman squinting at envelopes and muttering uncertainly.

It was not that Mama disliked the job itself—he admired the uniform, the sense of purpose in delivering important documents, and the possibility of a secure wage. However, the daily fear of messing up, combined with the weight of his family's hopes, became overwhelming. He had nightmares of a massive backlog of letters, each envelope a puzzle in an alien script.

One morning, Mama telephoned the post office from a public booth—a call that cost him one anna, a precious coin in his budget. Stammering slightly, he informed them that his mother was gravely ill in the village and he needed to rush home. He didn't know if the person on the other end believed him, but they noted his excuse. Mama then packed a small bag, taking only what he truly needed. Over the previous weeks, he had not even collected his first official salary, partly because the admin paperwork was incomplete and partly because he had not mustered the courage to ask.

Without a formal resignation or any written notice, Mama boarded a train heading back to his village in Ahmednagar district. Guilt weighed on him as he stared at the passing scenery. He thought of the uniform he left behind, the hopeful chatter of colleagues who had welcomed him. He thought of his wife, who had looked at him with concern but also relief—relief that he might step away from the relentless stress. The cityscape gave way to more rural landscapes, each station less crowded than the last, until he finally reached a point where small roads led to his ancestral home.

In the village, Mama's parents were surprised to see him. He offered a vague explanation about an urgent issue, but the entire story remained locked in his chest. Part of him felt he had failed a golden opportunity—something that might have changed his fortunes forever. The tension that had haunted him each morning in the sorting hall melted away, replaced by the simpler, if still impoverished, rhythms of village life.

Mama stayed in the village for several days, telling neighbors he was on leave. Deep inside, he knew he was unlikely to return to the post office. The thought of stepping back into that courtyard, of facing the supervisor's questions about his sudden absence, filled him with dread. And yet, he also knew that by walking away, he had forfeited what could have been a life-changing position. If only he had better literacy skills or more time to adapt, the outcome might have been different.

He tried to bury the regret by helping his father mend shoes and chappals in the village, a familiar chore from his childhood. Each day, they set up a small workspace, waiting for local farmers or passersby to drop off their worn footwear. Occasionally, Mama reflected on how many twists and turns his life had taken since he first came to Mumbai. Life in the village lacked the intensity of the city, but it also lacked the same opportunities. He felt caught between two worlds, neither of which truly fit him.

Eventually, Mama realized he needed to finalize matters. The post office might be expecting him to return or at least to send in some formal request for extended leave. But every time he thought about writing a letter, the literacy gap came back to haunt him. He could ask a friend to write on his behalf, but the idea still mortified him. Instead, he let inertia win. Weeks slid into a month, and he never returned to the Fort Post Office to collect any wage or finalize paperwork.

When local villagers asked about his city job, Mama gave polite, non-committal replies. Over time, they stopped asking. Life in the village resumed its slow, predictable patterns, and Mama's short-lived stint at the post office became a fading chapter—an interlude defined by hope, anxiety, and an abrupt end.

Though brief, Mama's post office experience left a lasting impact. He had proven his capacity to learn quickly—mastering the figure-8 bicycle test against all odds—yet he also confronted the harsh reality that certain barriers, like English illiteracy, were not easily overcome on short notice. The tension between his aspirations and the structural constraints of the job weighed heavily on him, forcing a tough decision to leave before the situation worsened.

In the broader context of Mama's journey, this episode underscores the limitations faced by many individuals from disadvantaged backgrounds. A person with grit, intelligence, and strong work ethic can still find themselves sidelined by formal requirements that do not account for cultural and educational gaps. The irony lies in Mama's demonstration of resilience—if given suitable support or a patient mentor, he might have excelled in the role. Instead, he slipped away in silence, returning to a village that offered fewer opportunities but more emotional safety.

For Mama, the experience also hinted at how close he had come to a more stable life. If only he could have conquered the language barrier, he might have built a career delivering mail, gaining a secure salary that could change his household's future. The "what if" lingered in his thoughts long after his final train ride away from the Fort Post Office. It became a reminder that luck and timing matter as much as personal effort, and that not every open door is easily passed through.

Mama's brief foray into the Fort Post Office was a classic tale of hope colliding with hard realities. An unexpected call to a government job—sparked by a humble employment card renewal—momentarily lifted his spirits and earned him the admiration of family and friends. The victory of passing the bicycle figure-8 test was a personal triumph, demonstrating his willingness to put in grueling late-night practice for a shot at respectable work.

Yet, the job itself demanded literacy skills and composure under pressure that Mama had not yet acquired. Day after day, handling letters in an unfamiliar language eroded his confidence, overshadowing the excitement of donning an official uniform. Unable to bridge the gap, Mama chose the path of least resistance: slipping back to the familiarity of his village rather than facing the possibility of constant reprimand or dismissal in the city.

This interlude thus became a poignant lesson in how ambition and capability are sometimes thwarted by systemic barriers and inadequate support. In the end, Mama's choice to leave was not so much a rejection of stable employment as it was an acceptance of his present limitations—limitations forged by deeply rooted social and educational inequalities. Though the disappointment ran deep, the episode added another layer to Mama's experience of the world: that not every chance, no matter how promising, can be seized without the right tools and environment.

72

CHAPTER NINE

SERVING AS A PEON IN THE VIDHAN SABHA (1961–1977)

For Sitaram "Mama" Ghandat, the opportunity to serve as a peon in the Maharashtra Vidhan Sabha marked a striking shift in his life's journey. After years of struggling for steady employment—experiencing fleeting roles, the turbulent Post Office interlude, and the constant hustle of cobbler work—he found a post that offered both stability and a window into the state's political corridors. Between 1961 and 1977, Mama's time at the Vidhan Sabha would shape his understanding of governance, build his confidence as he interacted with prominent leaders, and introduce a new set of housing struggles that tested his resilience.

Mama's entry into the Vidhan Sabha came shortly after the abrupt end of his Post Office job. Though the mail-delivery position had promised stability, it ultimately collapsed under the strain of language barriers and stress. Back in Mumbai, Mama returned to his makeshift routines—cobbler work, odd jobs, and occasional help from friends. But another door soon opened: through the same employment card system that had once linked him to the Post Office, Mama was informed of a new government vacancy.

This time, the position was for a peon (or office attendant) in the Maharashtra Vidhan Sabha. Given his limited formal education, Mama was cautiously optimistic. He understood that a peon's duties would likely be more straightforward than dealing with English addresses. On the appointed interview date, Mama arrived at the Vidhan Sabha building—an imposing structure that symbolized the authority of the state government. Clad in simple attire, he sat among a pool of candidates, all awaiting a chance to prove their suitability for the role.

The selection panel interviewed around 60 to 70 applicants for about 10 openings, according to Mama's recollection. Some came with more formal schooling, others boasted prior government experience, yet Mama suspected that his record of reliability and sincerity might stand out. During the interview, the officials posed basic questions: Was he comfortable assisting senior staff? Could he run errands, distribute documents, and handle menial tasks without complaint? Mama answered affirmatively, pointing to his history of hard work in the city. Perhaps, too, someone recognized his perseverance from his attempts at the Post Office or other government channels. In the end, he was among the lucky few selected.

As a peon, Mama's daily responsibilities revolved around attending to the logistical needs of various officials and MLAs (Members of the Legislative Assembly). Much of his work took place behind the scenes, ensuring that documents moved swiftly, refreshments reached meeting rooms on time, and urgent messages—often written hastily on paper slips or notes—were delivered across the assembly floors. One of the most symbolic tasks for a Vidhan Sabha peon was carrying these small notes from one office or MLA to another, even during active assembly sessions. Mama would dash between corridors, carefully safeguarding messages that ranged from voting instructions to private requests. Accuracy mattered, as a lost or delayed note could derail an important conversation or disrupt the scheduling of legislative business.

In addition to message-running, Mama played a crucial role in administrative support. He arranged files, fetched water or tea for MLAs, and sometimes helped set up seats or desks before sessions. The environment was always busy, punctuated by urgent phone calls, heated debates in the assembly halls, and the constant movement of political figures. Despite the pressure, Mama learned to maintain a calm demeanor. Politicians, deeply engrossed in passing bills or negotiating alliances, often needed errands completed swiftly. A composed and adaptable peon was invaluable in such a setting, and over time, Mama developed a reputation for being approachable, good-humored, and efficient.

With each interaction, his confidence grew. He began recognizing the faces of important MLAs, learning their routines, and exchanging polite greetings. A few kindly politicians asked him about his life, curious about how someone from a humble background had found his way into the Vidhan Sabha.

For 17 years, Mama found himself immersed in a world far removed from the chawl sidewalks. He had a front-row seat to the workings of democracy in Maharashtra, witnessing fierce debates on the assembly floor, behind-closed-door negotiations, and occasional conversations about policies that shaped the entire state. The Vidhan Sabha peon roster typically served under multiple governments, working with a rotating cast of chief ministers, assembly speakers, and party leaders. During Mama's era, he saw prominent figures like Yashwantrao Chavan, Vasantrao Naik, and other influential politicians who played a crucial role in shaping Maharashtra's policy landscape.

Mama's naturally extroverted personality caught the attention of many. His enthusiasm for assisting and his efficiency in delivering important chits made him a familiar face across party lines. Politicians from rival factions recognized him by name, appreciating his reliability and promptness. Beyond these interactions, Mama's time in the Vidhan Sabha gradually expanded his worldview. Witnessing lawmakers spar over public issues, he realized that government was not just a distant institution but a space where real decisions—impacting roads, water supply, and welfare programs—were actively debated. This growing awareness planted the seeds of his own political aspirations.

Yet, for all its glamour, the role of a peon remained behind the scenes. Mama had no official authority, and his daily wage did not miraculously lift him out of poverty. Even as he walked the polished corridors of power, he remained tethered to the same struggles of housing and finances that had shaped his early years.

During Mama's Vidhan Sabha tenure, the clash between his emerging stability and his precarious home life was stark. He had managed to claim a small patch of land in area where he erected a makeshift shelter. Fashioned from tar sheets and rudimentary materials, it was hardly a grand abode, but it shielded his wife and children from the elements.

However, the municipality viewed it as unauthorized dwellings and as targets for demolition. Repeatedly, large municipal trucks and demolition crews would arrive, threatening to dismantle the entire slum or sub-section where Mama's home stood. Each time this happened, Mama's wife would frantically reach out, sometimes sending word through neighbors or making a frantic phone call for one anna at a local booth. Mama, at the Vidhan Sabha, felt a deep pit of worry. He knew that if the bulldozers tore down their structure, his family would be homeless again.

On multiple occasions, Mama made desperate phone calls to acquaintances in the municipality or local leaders who had the clout to delay demolition. Sometimes, he used connections he had cultivated while delivering documents or chits in the Vidhan Sabha. A sympathetic official might call the municipal department to grant a temporary reprieve. Other times, Mama hurried home in the evening, consoling his distressed wife, patching up minor damage, and bracing for the next round of municipal action.

This cat-and-mouse game sapped Mama's peace of mind. He longed for a more legitimate housing solution. Each threat of eviction reminded him that, despite earning a stable government wage, he was not fully secure.

Fortune eventually smiled upon Mama in the form of high-level support. Among the many political figures Mama interacted with was V. S. Page—a respected leader who served as the Chairman (Sabhapati) of the Vidhan Parishad (Legislative Council), the upper house of Maharashtra's legislature. Through routine errands and interactions, Mama caught Page's attention. Perhaps it was Mama's diligence in delivering messages promptly, or his polite greetings in the corridors. Whatever the reason, Page began to see Mama as more than just a nameless peon.

It was not unusual for staffers or support workers to approach sympathetic legislators about personal struggles. In Mama's case, one of his friends—who delivered tiffins (home-cooked meals) to offices—had a connection to Page. Sensing Mama's desperation, the friend arranged a short meeting. Mama stepped into Page's office, somewhat timid, but determined to plead his case regarding the municipality's relentless demolition attempts.

During their brief exchange, Mama explained his circumstances with quiet urgency. He spoke about his family background, describing how he hailed from a marginalized community, lacked stable land in the village, and had come to Mumbai in search of a better life. His struggles did not end upon arriving in the city; instead, they took on new forms, particularly in the battle for secure housing. Repeated demolition notices meant living in constant fear of returning to homelessness, forcing him and his family to exist in a state of uncertainty.

He also emphasized his deep dependence on his earnings in the city. His job in the Vidhan Sabha was a lifeline, offering a rare sense of stability. However, if his home were to be razed, he would face immense challenges in commuting long distances or finding an affordable place to relocate. Such a disruption could jeopardize everything he had worked so hard to build, threatening not just his residence but also his livelihood.

Page, known for being accessible and empathetic toward staff, listened attentively. He recognized Mama's sincerity. Perhaps influenced by Mama's track record of honest work, Page assured him he would see what could be done. True to his word, Page used his authority or political network to communicate with municipal officials, effectively instructing them to stop demolishing Mama's shack.

This intervention, while far from legalizing Mama's land claim, created an unofficial buffer. Municipal crews either received direct orders or realized that harassing Mama's home might anger powerful figures in the Vidhan Sabha. As a result, Mama's shack avoided further demolitions. With some relief, Mama added more improvements—like a makeshift toilet—though small fines and neighborly complaints still surfaced from time to time.

This close call with eviction and the subsequent reprieve granted by high-ranking officials significantly boosted Mama's morale. For one, he gained a clearer appreciation for the power of relationships within government structures. This was not mere favoritism; it was a lesson in how genuine connections and respectful networking could make or break one's fortunes in a system rife with red tape.

Additionally, Mama's wife and children finally experienced greater stability. No longer scrambling to gather belongings whenever a municipal truck approached, they could invest small sums in improving the shack's infrastructure. A steady supply of electricity, limited but functional water connections, and basic sanitation turned what was once a vulnerable shelter into a permanent fixture.

At the Vidhan Sabha, Mama carried himself with renewed confidence. Colleagues might ask how his housing issue was faring, and he could gratefully mention how an intervention from senior leadership eased the burden. Still, he remained cautious, aware that his home's legal status was far from settled. Any political upheaval or new municipal policy shift could rekindle threats of demolition. For now, though, he savored the reprieve, trusting that as long as he served diligently, figures like V. S. Page would stand by him.

From 1961 to 1977, the years passed as Mama steadily built experience and rapport in the Vidhan Sabha. He remained a silent witness to shifting party leadership, budgets passed for major infrastructure projects, and intense debates over land reforms, industrial development, and welfare schemes. Each session deepened his understanding of Maharashtra's political climate, exposing him to the intricate workings of governance.

Over nearly two decades, Mama became a recognized face among assembly members. He was the dependable peon who ensured chits were delivered on time, never losing them in the daily chaos. His friendly greetings became an ordinary yet reassuring presence in the otherwise hectic legislative environment. More than just a messenger, he absorbed the rhythm of governance, observing how MLAs tabled motions, formed alliances, and strategically negotiated across party lines. He realized that real change required more than just good intentions—it demanded careful planning, collaboration, and precise timing.

Though Mama rarely spoke about it, his years in the Vidhan Sabha sparked something within him. Being so close to power made him wonder whether someone from his background could aspire to more than just a supporting role. Could he, one day, engage in social or political work himself? These thoughts were still unformed, mere seeds of ambition, but with time, they would take root and shape his future in unexpected ways.

Meanwhile, his family in the chawl grew. Mama and his wife welcomed children—sons and a daughter—who played in the lanes around their improved shack. The small salary from the Vidhan Sabha, though not lavish, allowed Mama to consistently purchase essentials. He ensured his children at least had the chance to attend local schools, hoping they wouldn't face the same limitations he endured.

No journey is free of complications. Mama's siblings, who sometimes resented or misunderstood his life in the city, occasionally quarreled over inherited responsibilities. He also faced friction from local residents near his shack who disliked the special treatment that allowed his dwelling to remain untouched. Some muttered that Mama had used political influence unfairly. Others attempted to piggyback on his connections, asking him to speak on their behalf. Mama walked a tightrope—sympathetic to neighbors' struggles but hesitant to overextend his still-fragile political ties.

Additionally, Mama's own sense of self-worth fluctuated. On one hand, he felt pride working in a government institution, wearing a staff badge, and greeting senior officials daily. On the other, he remained mindful that he was a peon, not a policy-maker or an MLA. Sometimes, the stark difference between his humble living conditions and the more comfortable lifestyles of leaders made him question whether true upward mobility was possible.

But each time these doubts surfaced, Mama recalled how far he had come: from sleeping at Bus Stop No. 44 to holding a recognized role in the Vidhan Sabha. This progress, albeit incremental, underscored the value of persistence and the importance of forging respectful relationships.

Reflecting on his 17-year stint in the Vidhan Sabha, Mama would later pinpoint key lessons that shaped his perspective on work, society, and personal ambition. One of the most crucial realizations was the importance of networks. Government institutions could be labyrinthine, and navigating them effectively often required personal ties and goodwill. Mama's positive rapport with MLAs and staff, culminating in the help he received from V. S. Page, directly protected his home when it was under threat. These relationships reinforced the power of human connections in overcoming bureaucratic hurdles.

Another lesson was the dignity in service. While some might dismiss the role of a peon as menial, Mama took pride in executing his tasks well. He discovered that consistent effort, done with integrity, could open doors—if not always to formal promotions, then at least to personal growth and respect. His dependability earned him recognition, proving that any job, when done with commitment, carried its own worth.

Beyond the day-to-day work, Mama's exposure to larger causes left a lasting impact. Being surrounded by legislative discussions, he realized that laws and policies shaped the everyday realities of people like him. This insight fueled a growing conviction that real change might require direct participation—whether in politics or social work. Watching lawmakers debate issues of land, employment, and welfare, he began to see the connection between governance and the struggles of common people.

At the same time, balancing work and family remained a constant challenge. Mama's relentless schedule—delivering notes in the Vidhan Sabha, mending shoes on the side for extra income, and rushing home to prevent demolition—was a test of endurance. It demanded resourcefulness and reminded him that stability was fragile, something that had to be fiercely protected. These years laid the foundation for the resilience and determination that would define his future journey.

Although he might not have consciously planned it, Mama's time in the Vidhan Sabha laid the groundwork for future political aspirations. Seeing the mechanics of law-making demystified the process. He realized that the individuals leading the state were, at the end of the day, human beings—some approachable, some not, but all part of an intricate system where alliances and personal integrity mattered.

From 1961 to 1977, Mama's service as a peon in the Maharashtra Vidhan Sabha provided him with a rare vantage point into governance and political life. His consistent presence in the halls of power, rushing around with notes in hand, allowed him to become more than a faceless staff member. Over time, he earned the trust and goodwill of prominent leaders, most notably V. S. Page, whose intervention staved off municipal demolitions that threatened Mama's home.

These years were anything but easy. Mama juggled meager wages, municipal harassment, and the pressing need to provide for a growing family. Nonetheless, the Vidhan Sabha period stands out as a time of personal evolution. Each day's work, each interaction with legislative figures, strengthened his resolve. He discovered that while the system seemed vast and intimidating, it was also navigable with persistence and genuine rapport.

By the time he left the Vidhan Sabha in 1977, Mama had amassed invaluable knowledge about the inner workings of state politics, forged connections with influential individuals, and secured a degree of housing stability that once seemed impossible. The modest job title of "peon" did not capture the depth of experience he gained or the seeds it planted for his future. Indeed, the same resilience that had once kept him afloat as a cobbler and a day laborer now shaped him into a confident, resourceful individual who would soon embark on new chapters—ones that took him beyond the backrooms of government offices and into the dynamic world of active political participation.

CHAPTER TEN

GROWING POLITICAL AWARENESS

For Sitaram "Mama" Ghandat, politics had once seemed like a distant domain—something that only wealthier or more educated individuals could afford to engage in. But during his years as a peon in the Maharashtra Vidhan Sabha, Mama's life underwent a subtle yet profound transformation. The environment at the Assembly exposed him to the state's powerbrokers, taught him the mechanics of governance, and lit within him the first sparks of political aspiration. Yet his development into a politically conscious individual did not solely depend on what he witnessed at work. For three to four years, Mama also engaged with the Rashtriya Swayamsevak Sangh (RSS) shakha, a pathway that provided him with broader ideological insights and introduced him to influential leaders.

In this chapter, we explore the awakening of Mama's political awareness and the lessons he absorbed from prominent figures—some associated with the Sangh or with other political streams altogether. These encounters laid the groundwork for his eventual shift from behind-the-scenes roles into active participation in local and later state-level politics.

Mama's introduction to the RSS shakha was both spontaneous and reflective of how everyday social circles could lead him toward new beliefs. Many of his Vidhan Sabha colleagues and neighbors attended shakha gatherings in the mornings, often held in open grounds or municipal parks. Observers might see men and young boys dressed in simple uniforms—khaki shorts and white shirts—engaged in physical drills, exercises, and the recitation of patriotic chants.

At first, Mama attended the shakha out of curiosity, nudged by a few friends who suggested that it instilled discipline and offered moral teachings. What began as a casual visit soon turned into a routine, and over the next three to four years, Mama regularly attended these sessions. He discovered an environment that blended physical fitness with ideological discussions, emphasizing Indian cultural values, community unity, and a deep sense of national pride.

Mornings at the shakha typically began with daily drills, including exercises, marching routines, and group games aimed at building physical endurance. Having never engaged in structured sports before, Mama found the discipline refreshing. These physical activities were followed by *prarthana* and discussions, where participants reflected on self-improvement, social responsibilities, and India's historical heroes. Informal yet thought-provoking conversations covered a range of topics, from moral conduct to current events, gradually fostering Mama's budding sense of civic engagement.

Despite his limited literacy, Mama absorbed the ideological perspectives that the Sangh promoted—strengthening society from the grassroots, championing cultural unity, and defending the nation's diverse heritage. Whether one agreed or disagreed with certain stances, the shakha undeniably provided a platform that stimulated a strong sense of belonging and activism. For Mama, it was more than just a routine; it was an introduction to structured thought, discipline, and the realization that collective action had the potential to shape society.

This experience, Mama realized, complemented what he was learning at the Vidhan Sabha. Whereas his peon role gave him a pragmatic education in governance, the RSS shakha offered him a philosophical and cultural framework, encouraging him to consider how local communities could be organized around shared values. Though Mama would later chart his own political path, these formative sessions served as an early compass, teaching him that politics involved more than just policy—it was about identity, community, and moral grounding.

If the shakha meetings hinted at broad ideological possibilities, the Vidhan Sabha brought Mama face-to-face with seasoned politicians, activists, and cultural icons. Over the years, he crossed paths with individuals who had shaped Maharashtra's social and literary landscape, each leaving a lasting imprint on his mind. Some leaders stood out not just for their political stature but for the values they embodied, giving Mama deeper insight into the human side of leadership.

One such figure was Sayaji Rao Silam, known for his unwavering dedication to public service. Silam often greeted Mama with a friendly nod or a brief chat, and through these small yet meaningful interactions, Mama grasped how a leader could appear commanding in the assembly yet warm and approachable in private. It underscored the human element of politics, showing that leadership was not just about authority but also about connection.

Similarly, S. M. Joshi, a prominent socialist leader and advocate for labor rights, left an impression despite limited direct interactions. Mama often handed over notes or documents to Joshi and observed his compassionate demeanor toward staffers. Joshi never ignored a greeting, a simple gesture that spoke volumes about his respect for people regardless of their position. His ability to balance ideological fervor with personal kindness inspired Mama, reinforcing the idea that true leadership extended beyond political rhetoric.

Among the most striking personalities was Acharya Atre, a legendary journalist, writer, and orator known for his sharp wit and fearless criticism of wrongdoing. Though Mama rarely spoke to him directly, merely watching Atre in action within the legislative arena was an education in itself. Atre's speeches blended humor, intellect, and bold critique, making Mama realize that political influence wasn't limited to those holding office—it could also be wielded through the power of words.

Another key figure was G. D. Madgulkar, primarily recognized as a writer and lyricist. His presence in policy-making circles revealed to Mama the profound connection between cultural creativity and politics. On more than one occasion, Mama delivered notes to Madgulkar, struck by how even poets and lyricists could shape public discourse and policy decisions. It was a reminder that ideas—whether expressed through legislation or literature—could mold society.

Ram Babu Mhalgi, known for his grassroots activism, had an equally strong impact on Mama. Mhalgi's commitment to engaging directly with local communities emphasized that real progress began at the bottom. Mama, having grown up in a world where survival often depended on collective effort, resonated deeply with this approach. It reinforced his belief that leadership was most effective when it prioritized people's immediate needs rather than abstract political maneuvering.

The presence of Bapu Kaldate further reinforced this notion. A strong advocate for socio-political reforms, Kaldate displayed both a strategic mind and a sincere commitment to uplifting marginalized communities. Whenever Mama delivered documents to his office, he observed how methodically Kaldate approached issues, breaking them down to their core. This blend of practicality and empathy appealed to Mama's growing understanding of leadership—good governance, he realized, required both knowledge and compassion.

Finally, Krishna Rao Dhulap, a leader known for his strong administrative skills, left an impression on Mama through his meticulous approach to organization and punctuality. Watching Dhulap at work reinforced the value of discipline, a principle that Mama himself had begun to embrace in his own responsibilities—whether delivering legislative papers on time or maintaining focus during shakha drills.

Each of these encounters added another layer to Mama's evolving perspective. The Vidhan Sabha was not just a workplace; it was a space where he absorbed lessons in leadership, discipline, and social impact. These figures, though operating on different ideological spectrums, all contributed to shaping his understanding of the world—and, unknowingly, helped sow the seeds of his own future aspirations.

These glimpses into leadership provided Mama with a valuable takeaway: political stature did not manifest in a vacuum. Each of these men seemed driven by distinctive ideologies, personal convictions, and a capacity to interact respectfully with others. Over the years, Mama pieced together an informal "leadership handbook" from these observations. He learned that public trust often hinged on humility, consistency, and the ability to communicate sincerely—qualities he strove to cultivate in himself.

Mama's RSS involvement and exposure to Vidhan Sabha luminaries naturally planted ideas about whether he, too, could create change. Initially, the notion felt audacious. Mama lacked formal education, lacked wealth, and came from a historically marginalized background. Yet the synergy of experiences stirred a quiet conviction that ordinary people could indeed enter the political arena if they possessed unwavering resolve.

This realization was not driven by power or personal gain but by a deep-seated desire to address the everyday struggles he witnessed. Mama saw how municipal authorities repeatedly threatened slum demolitions, how workers fought for fair wages, and how families suffered due to inadequate water and sanitation. The thought that political engagement might provide solutions to these issues slowly took shape in his mind.

His experiences at the *shakha* played a role in this transformation. The RSS circle often hosted discussions on social injustices, moral responsibilities, and the qualities of strong leadership. While Mama did not always agree with every viewpoint, he found these debates illuminating. He internalized the core principle that a cohesive society required active citizens—people willing to speak up for better policies and fight for the collective good.

Similarly, his years in the Vidhan Sabha offered a firsthand view of how governance operated. Watching intense debates on land reforms, labor rights, and public welfare, he saw that legislation had the power to reshape society. He observed MLAs who fought for bills to protect vulnerable communities and realized that policies, when effectively framed, could directly improve lives. This led him to reason that someone with his lived experiences—someone who truly understood the struggles of ordinary people—might one day be able to advocate for the voiceless in a way that others could not.

What began as an unshaped thought slowly crystallized into a conviction: real change required participation, and he could no longer remain just an observer.

Additionally, Mama met individuals through the Vidhan Sabha or shakha who urged him not to shy away from broader participation. Some older staffers, seeing his integrity and empathy, half-jokingly prodded: "When will we see you as a corporator or MLA?" Mama brushed off such remarks with a laugh, but deep down, he mulled over the possibility. He recognized that genuine leadership was less about lofty speeches and more about understanding the hardships people faced every day—an area where Mama considered himself an expert by necessity.

The synergy of professional and ideological influences nudged Mama to look beyond the peon's uniform and see himself as someone with a voice, albeit not yet a prominent one. Engaging with RSS shakha activities crystallized values like discipline, community solidarity, and a focus on cultural identity. Meanwhile, the connections formed in the Vidhan Sabha taught him that alliances could be built across party lines if one was earnest, respectful, and solution-driven.

Through these transformations, Mama navigated an evolving sense of self, gradually shaping his outlook and abilities. His confidence grew through routine participation in both the *shakha* and his daily responsibilities at the Vidhan Sabha. Regular involvement in these spaces taught him to speak up—whether it was clarifying a detail with an MLA or offering input on small community issues in his neighborhood. What had once seemed intimidating became second nature, reinforcing his belief that his voice mattered.

Alongside confidence, he developed networking skills that would later prove invaluable. Mama began extending his circle, engaging in casual yet meaningful conversations. He exchanged a few extra words with a local organizer at the *shakha* or a political worker in the Assembly who needed help delivering documents. These interactions, though seemingly minor at the time, laid the groundwork for a future political network—one built not on opportunism but on genuine recognition of Mama's sincerity and reliability.

Perhaps most significantly, Mama refined his moral compass through exposure to diverse political perspectives. The *shakha* emphasized nationalist and cultural ideals, while the Vidhan Sabha introduced him to the complexities of governance, where inclusivity and negotiation were essential. Rather than adopting a rigid stance, Mama balanced these influences, absorbing what resonated with his personal sense of fairness and empathy. He came to understand that true leadership was not about blind allegiance to ideology but about making decisions rooted in justice and practical solutions for the people he sought to serve.

At times, Mama felt torn. The RSS platform championed certain cultural narratives that clashed with the more secular or socialist perspectives embraced by some leaders in the Assembly. But Mama refused to limit himself to a single ideological lane. Instead, he absorbed what he considered valuable from all sides, shaping his own balanced stance. This open-mindedness later became an asset, allowing him to work with diverse political factions.

A typical day for Mama during these formative years reflected his dual identity—balancing his ideological engagement at the *shakha* with his professional responsibilities at the Vidhan Sabha. His routine was structured yet dynamic, offering him exposure to both grassroots activism and the corridors of political power.

His pre-dawn start began with a disciplined morning routine as he made his way to the local park or open ground for *shakha* activities. There, he engaged in physical exercises, offered prayers, and participated in brief philosophical or historical discussions led by senior RSS volunteers. These sessions instilled discipline and a sense of purpose, reinforcing his growing awareness of social and national issues.

After an hour or two at the *shakha*, he transitioned to work, hurrying home to freshen up. A quick meal or tea, often prepared by his wife, fueled him for the day ahead. If time allowed, he checked on his children, ensuring they were ready for school before setting off for the Vidhan Sabha.

At the Vidhan Sabha, Mama seamlessly stepped into his duties—sorting and delivering important documents, greeting MLAs at their desks, and moving between offices to complete various errands. Over lunch breaks, he engaged in conversations with peers and officials, discussing the day's legislative agenda and absorbing insights into political strategies. These informal interactions gave him a deeper understanding of governance and policy-making, far beyond what was visible to the public.

After work, his post-session chores and networking further strengthened his connections. On non-session days, he often ran errands for influential leaders, delivered typed notes to ministers' residences, or completed small tasks that fostered goodwill. Through these efforts, Mama built a reputation as someone dependable and resourceful, gradually expanding his personal network among political and administrative circles.

The evening brought reflection, a quiet moment after the day's whirlwind of activity. Over a simple dinner with his wife, he often shared highlights from his day. "Do you know," he'd say, "I delivered a letter to S. M. Joshi, who was discussing labor laws." Or, "At the *shakha* this morning, we talked about self-reliance." These conversations, though seemingly ordinary, marked his slow but steady immersion into a life of political and ideological awareness. Every experience, from delivering messages to witnessing legislative debates, was shaping his understanding of leadership, service, and social change.

This delicate balance—juggling a physically demanding job with intellectual and spiritual inputs—contributed to Mama's well-rounded approach to problem-solving. He appreciated the practicality demanded by governance and the ideals championed in cultural or moral frameworks, forging a nuanced perspective that appealed to people from varied backgrounds.

Beyond formal tasks, Mama's political consciousness grew through countless minor encounters that seldom make headlines but matter immensely. An assembly staffer might invite him to a family function where local politicians were present, and Mama's polite conversation there could open future doors. Or, a shakha colleague might mention a civic issue—like a broken water pipeline or a neglected road—that needed collective attention. Mama, bridging these two worlds, relayed such concerns to an MLA who genuinely cared.

These instances, modest though they were, gave Mama an inkling of how real change sometimes germinated from small seeds. He began to see himself as a conduit, linking the gritty realities of slum dwellers, daily wage earners, or youth in the shakha to those who held levers of power. This bridging role, though informal, planted the idea that politics was not about self-glorification but about forging connections that result in tangible benefits for the underprivileged.

Although Mama had not yet formally declared his intention to enter politics, the seeds of ambition were undeniably sown by the late 1960s to early 1970s. He witnessed men of action addressing real-world problems, analyzing them through an ideological lens, and persuading others to join their cause. It reinforced the idea that with enough dedication, someone of humble origin could also step up—especially since Mama's daily life was a testament to the challenges ordinary people faced.

The stage was set: Mama possessed a unique vantage point (courtesy of his Vidhan Sabha peon role), a supportive moral framework (imbibed from the RSS shakha), and a personal story that resonated with countless underprivileged families. Over time, his confidence in bridging formal politics and grassroots realities only expanded. Soon, small gestures—like delivering messages or raising local issues—would take on larger significance as Mama moved toward a position where he could champion issues himself, rather than simply relaying them to others.

If the Post Office interlude and the subsequent Vidhan Sabha years had taught Mama perseverance, these new experiences with the RSS and varied state leaders honed his sense of purpose. He was transforming from an observer of politics into someone who might one day shape it. While that journey was still fraught with uncertainties—financial constraints, social biases, and fierce competition from established figures—Mama's quiet assurance grew stronger with each passing conversation and every glance at the debates swirling around him.

CHAPTER ELEVEN

ENTRY INTO ACTIVE POLITICS: JAN SANGH TO BJP

Sitaram "Mama" Ghandat's political awareness began developing quietly through his work as a peon in the Maharashtra Vidhan Sabha and his attendance at RSS shakha sessions. These early experiences planted the seeds of public service in his mind, but he had not yet taken a decisive step into active politics. That transition began when he met Vamanrao Parab, a key figure who introduced him to the Jan Sangh, which later became the Bharatiya Janata Party. Mama started with small organizational tasks like putting up posters, managing local meetings, and gathering memberships, gradually immersing himself in the political movement that would shape his future.

Vamanrao Parab played a crucial role in Mama's transition from an interested observer to an active party worker. Parab was well known for his organizational skills and ability to connect with ordinary people. He was constantly searching for energetic newcomers who might not have political privilege but possessed a passion for public service. Through mutual acquaintances, possibly from the Vidhan Sabha or the RSS shakha, Mama and Parab crossed paths. Their discussions revolved around Mama's background, his experiences growing up in a chawl, his struggles with municipal authorities, and his understanding of the challenges faced by working-class neighborhoods. Recognizing Mama's deep grassroots knowledge and his ability to relate to people, Parab saw great potential in him. Unlike political elites, Mama had firsthand experience of the hardships of slum dwellers, making him an ideal advocate if given the right guidance.

Encouraged by Parab's invitation, Mama hesitantly joined Jan Sangh. He had no prior experience with formal party structures, and the idea of local campaigning felt unfamiliar. However, Parab's sincerity and the opportunity to channel his community-level insights into practical work convinced him to step forward. Once Mama joined, Parab wasted no time in assigning him basic organizational responsibilities. Though seemingly trivial to outsiders, these tasks formed the backbone of any grassroots movement. Mama had to balance late-night poster work, collecting membership fees, and attending strategy meetings, all while managing his job and family obligations. Despite the challenges, he embraced the work, understanding that true political engagement begins at the ground level.

One of his earliest tasks was putting up party posters in crowded neighborhoods. At first, it seemed like mere physical labor, but he soon realized the importance of visibility in political outreach. For people who did not read newspapers or attend rallies, posters served as their first connection to a party's presence. Due to limited funds, workers had to be resourceful, often using homemade adhesives made from boiled water, flour, and mashed banana pulp. Mama and his fellow volunteers would stir pots of this mixture and carry buckets of glue through the streets, their hands and clothes covered in the sticky paste. Despite the mess, Mama found humor in the experience, often joking that politics starts with the sticky work.

Beyond fieldwork, Mama attended daily meetings where strategies were discussed, including poster placements, membership drives, and addressing community concerns like water shortages and sanitation. These discussions also served as his informal political education, where he learned about Jan Sangh's ideology, which emphasized nationalism, cultural values, and social unity. At the same time, his interactions with slum residents and factory workers brought real-world perspectives to the table. One of his more direct responsibilities was collecting party memberships, a task that required persuasion and patience. The membership fee was minimal, but it symbolized a commitment to the party's vision. Mama would walk through narrow lanes, knocking on doors, explaining the party's agenda, and encouraging people to sign up. Some agreed easily, while others demanded proof of what the party had done for them. Initially, Mama struggled to answer all their concerns, but with time, he developed the confidence to articulate the party's goals and address people's grievances effectively.

By 1980, Jan Sangh transformed into the Bharatiya Janata Party under national leaders like L. K. Advani. This transition brought both excitement and challenges for ground-level workers. In Mumbai, Jan Sangh loyalists quickly adapted to the new identity, hoping to broaden the party's reach. One of the key neighborhoods for establishing a BJP presence was Parel, an area historically associated with textile mills and working-class families. Mama and his colleagues recognized that this region was home to thousands of potential voters who felt neglected by mainstream parties. If the BJP wanted to establish itself in Mumbai, it needed to secure a base in industrial and slum-heavy areas like Parel.

With encouragement from Parab, Mama played a vital role in securing a small office for the BJP in Parel. It was not a grand establishment—just a modest ground-floor space with a broken signboard and dusty walls. However, for local party supporters, it was a symbol of presence. Mama and volunteers took on the manual labor of cleaning, repairing leaks, and whitewashing the walls. They installed simple wooden benches and prominently displayed the BJP's lotus emblem outside. More than just an office, it became a space for community engagement.

To draw people in, the team organized small yet impactful events such as free medical check-ups, children's activities, and informal gatherings where BJP pamphlets were distributed. Mama believed in keeping the office open and accessible to everyone, regardless of political affiliation. The goal was not just to build party support but to establish a place where people could seek guidance on bureaucratic matters. Over time, the office became a hub of daily activity, with Mama spending long hours there, listening to residents' problems, helping with official paperwork, and guiding them on how to approach municipal authorities. These efforts turned the BJP office into more than just a political base—it became a community resource.

As Mama's presence grew, his dedication to serving people became widely recognized. His reliability made him a trusted figure among locals, and his name became synonymous with problem-solving. Whether collecting membership fees, answering public queries, or accompanying worried residents to government offices, Mama handled each task with quiet efficiency. His tireless efforts made people feel that someone genuinely cared about their concerns. He also mentored younger volunteers, encouraging them to approach strangers for memberships and navigate the challenges of grassroots politics. His patient guidance helped build a stronger team spirit among BJP workers.

Campaign work remained an essential part of grassroots politics. Every election cycle required a renewed effort to plaster posters across walls and bus stops. Many activists had shifted to printing professional banners, but for small-scale outreach, cost-effective methods were still necessary. Mama and his team often conducted late-night poster runs, carrying buckets of homemade glue through the streets of Parel. The technique of using banana pulp adhesive became their signature method, ensuring posters remained firmly attached even during Mumbai's monsoons. These efforts were not just about visibility; they allowed Mama to engage with people directly, gather public opinions, and refine the party's outreach strategies.

Mama's increasing involvement in politics also expanded his influence beyond Parel. His dedication caught the attention of senior party leaders, earning him invitations to city-level meetings and rally planning sessions. At the same time, his ability to connect with ordinary people reinforced the BJP's credibility in working-class neighborhoods. His interactions with slum dwellers and shop owners made the BJP office in Parel a trusted place for resolving civic issues. His growing responsibilities required him to refine his communication skills, mediate disputes, and navigate the complexities of grassroots politics.

While he had not yet considered running for office, Mama realized that true political influence required active participation. The recurring grievances he encountered—water shortages, eviction threats, and neglected infrastructure—highlighted the need for representation. Although he remained focused on building the BJP's local foundation, the idea of standing for elections began taking shape in his mind.

Over time, Mama's work earned him a distinct reputation in the community. People who once ignored Jan Sangh now recognized its efforts, largely due to the support system he had helped build. If someone needed help with legal paperwork, eviction notices, or municipal processes, Mama helped them with that. This trust, built through consistent action rather than political rhetoric, cemented his role as a dependable figure.

Mama's journey into politics, from a hesitant volunteer to a dedicated grassroots organizer, was marked by hard work and unwavering commitment. What began with simple tasks like pasting posters and running membership drives gradually evolved into a leadership role within the party. His ability to connect with people, understand their struggles, and provide tangible solutions turned him into a trusted local leader. His story was no longer about supporting a movement; it was about actively shaping it, one step at a time.

CHAPTER TWELVE

First Political Contest: A Leap of Faith (1977–78)

By the late 1970s, Sitaram "Mama" Ghandat had spent years balancing humble employment with growing political involvement. As a peon in the Maharashtra Vidhan Sabha, he quietly absorbed lessons on governance while building relationships. His association with Jan Sangh, later the Bharatiya Janata Party, allowed him to develop grassroots organizing skills, such as distributing posters, conducting membership drives, and establishing a small local office in Parel. Despite these experiences, he had never contested an election. That changed in 1977–78 when senior political figures urged him to resign from his government job and stand for municipal elections. It was an exciting but daunting prospect, a decision that could elevate his standing or result in a crushing defeat.

For years, Mama had been an active party worker, attending daily meetings and engaging in local political work. He had built strong connections across Mumbai neighborhoods, earning a reputation for hard work and sincerity. Senior leaders within the Jan Sangh-BJP recognized qualities in him that could translate into electoral success—his relatability with working-class voters, his willingness to tackle unglamorous tasks, and his firsthand understanding of governance from his Vidhan Sabha experience. As the municipal elections neared, these leaders saw an opportunity to expand the party's presence, particularly in the Lalbaug-Parel area, where Mama was deeply engaged. However, his government job posed a challenge. Contesting an election required full-time campaigning, extensive public engagement, and flexibility to attend rallies. Managing both responsibilities simultaneously was impractical.

Mama struggled with the decision to resign. His government job provided a stable income and a sense of belonging he had worked hard to earn. Leaving it meant stepping into uncertainty with no guarantee of success. Yet, the possibility of directly influencing local governance—ensuring better slum rehabilitation, improving water supply, and addressing community issues—was a powerful motivation. After discussions with his wife, who was both concerned and supportive, he made the difficult choice to step down. Handing in his resignation was an emotional moment. He had been a familiar presence in the Assembly for nearly two decades, and colleagues expressed mixed reactions, some encouraging his political aspirations, others warning of the risks. His supervisor gave him a parting word of encouragement, hoping that the qualities he demonstrated in service would be recognized by the public. Mama left the Vidhan Sabha with a final paycheck and no backup plan should his election bid fail.

With no job to fall back on, Mama dedicated himself fully to his campaign. His constituency covered Lalbaug and Parel, areas populated by mill workers and densely packed chawls. Campaigning required more than political speeches; it required trust-building through direct engagement. Mama revisited slum pockets where he had previously helped residents fight evictions, spoke to shopkeepers about their struggles, and interacted with factory workers to understand their concerns. His message was straightforward—he was not just a party candidate but someone who had lived these challenges and was committed to solving them.

As the campaign gained momentum, posters bearing Mama's name and face appeared across the constituency. Seeing his own face on election materials was a new and somewhat uncomfortable experience, but he understood the importance of visibility. His team designed a simple, direct slogan to resonate with voters: "Safe Homes, Clean Water, Honest Leaders." This message, tied to practical solutions, became the foundation of his outreach.

Despite his local presence, Mama faced stiff competition. Established political parties had strong campaign machinery, well-funded outreach, and the ability to offer small incentives to voters. Mama's campaign was modest in comparison, relying more on personal goodwill than financial resources. Each day, he woke early to distribute handbills and meet voters at bus stops, markets, and residential areas. While some people warmly supported him, recalling his past community work, others were skeptical of any new candidate. Many voters had seen election promises before, only to be disappointed once leaders were elected. Mama had to reassure them that he was different, that his involvement would not end after the votes were counted.

One of the most daunting challenges of the campaign was public speaking. His party arranged a rally at Lal Maidan, where he was expected to address a large crowd. Although he had spoken in small group settings before, standing before hundreds of people with a microphone in hand was an entirely new experience. As he stood backstage watching seasoned politicians deliver speeches with confidence, his nervousness grew. When his name was called, he stepped onto the stage, feeling the weight of the moment. He began tentatively, thanking the audience and highlighting key issues like demolitions, water shortages, and daily hardships. However, as he tried to transition into policy points, his mind went blank. The words on his speech paper blurred, and a heavy silence filled the air. A few supporters clapped in encouragement, but the nervousness refused to subside. Overwhelmed, Mama cut his speech short and stepped away from the podium, apologizing softly into the microphone.

The rally ended with mixed reactions. Some in the crowd sympathized, understanding his nervousness as a first-time speaker, while others saw it as a sign of inexperience. For Mama, the moment was deeply humiliating. That night, he struggled with self-doubt, replaying the scene in his mind. Had he let his supporters down? Would this one incident overshadow all the work he had done? Senior colleagues reassured him that even experienced politicians faced such difficulties, urging him not to give up. But the memory of that faltering speech remained a reminder of how much he needed to grow in public presentation.

Despite the setback, his campaign continued until election day. Volunteers intensified door-to-door visits, distributing leaflets and emphasizing Mama's genuine commitment to the people. Mama himself focused on solving immediate problems, such as helping residents file complaints about water supply issues or eviction threats. Yet, when the votes were counted, the result was disappointing—he lost to a better-funded and more established candidate.

The defeat was more than a political loss; it left Mama jobless and uncertain about the future. With no steady income, financial pressure mounted at home. Some well-wishers who had encouraged him to contest now questioned whether the gamble had been worth it. The loss stung, not just because of the election outcome but because it also meant an uncertain livelihood. He had poured his energy into the campaign, sacrificing stability for a chance at public service, only to come up short. The experience also revealed the harsh realities of electoral politics—hard work and goodwill were not always enough to win against financial power and party machinery.

In the weeks that followed, Mama reflected on his next steps. Some supporters urged him to stay active in politics, reminding him that many leaders faced multiple defeats before achieving success. Others suggested that he step away and focus on rebuilding his livelihood. He needed to provide for his family, but he also knew that walking away from politics entirely was not an option. He considered practical solutions, such as becoming a rented taxi driver to earn a living while remaining involved in party activities. This would allow him financial independence while continuing his work for the community.

Through this period of self-reflection, Mama recognized the lessons his first election had taught him. He had learned that winning required more than sincerity—it required preparation, strong messaging, and the ability to connect with voters on a larger scale. He understood that his biggest challenge was public speaking, and if he ever wanted to contest again, he had to overcome this weakness. Friends encouraged him to participate in local debates, community discussions, and even smaller press interactions to build confidence.

Despite the disappointment, Mama's resolve remained intact. The election loss did not erase the relationships he had built or the community trust he had earned. He knew now that political success was a long journey requiring resilience, learning, and repeated effort. While he had lost this contest, he had gained invaluable experience that would shape his future strategies. Rather than an ending, the defeat marked a beginning—a stepping stone toward a future in which he would be better prepared, stronger, and more determined.

As the months passed, Mama remained a visible presence in BJP circles. Though no longer a candidate, he continued assisting in recruitment drives, resolving civic issues, and mentoring younger volunteers. His name still carried weight in local discussions, and his dedication to public service was undeniable. The path forward was uncertain, but one thing was clear—he was not done yet. The lessons of this election had only strengthened his determination to continue fighting for the people he had always served.

CHAPTER THIRTEEN

TAXI DRIVER YEARS AND STEADFAST DETERMINATION

After losing his first municipal election and parting ways with a secure job in the Vidhan Sabha, Sitaram "Mama" Ghandat found himself at a crossroads. Though the defeat stung, it did not extinguish his growing passion for public service. Instead, it emboldened him to keep searching for ways to earn a living while sustaining his commitment to the Bharatiya Janata Party. Over the following years, Mama embarked on an unexpected journey as a taxi driver—an occupation that provided financial stability while allowing him the flexibility to continue his political engagement. This period saw his transformation from a single taxi renter to the owner of a fleet of seven. It was a phase of immense struggle, but one that shaped his leadership skills, sharpened his political acumen, and deepened his connection with the working-class people he aspired to represent. Despite facing yet another heartbreaking election defeat—this time by a mere 57 votes—Mama's resilience remained unshaken. His steady rise through various party ranks, coupled with his growing public presence, cemented his reputation as a leader admired by both passengers and party colleagues.

The defeat in the municipal election left Mama unemployed and uncertain. Having resigned from his government job to focus on his campaign, he now needed a way to support his family while maintaining his political involvement. Determined to avoid menial labor that would consume his time and limit his public work, he turned to taxi driving, a profession that allowed independence and flexibility. With no immediate means to buy a vehicle, he started by renting a black-and-yellow taxi, paying a daily fee to the owner. After covering the rental and fuel costs, he earned a modest but steady income. More importantly, he had control over his schedule, which meant he could pause his shifts to attend BJP meetings, assist residents with municipal paperwork, or engage in political activities. Though the profession was physically demanding, it provided a lifeline that allowed him to remain visible in the community and continue serving the people.

Driving a taxi in Mumbai came with its own set of challenges. The relentless traffic, long hours, and erratic weather tested his patience and endurance. He often began his day before sunrise, ferrying office-goers and factory workers to their destinations before taking a break to engage in party activities. By late evening, he was back on the road, trying to make up for lost earnings. The exhaustion was constant, but the job also presented unique opportunities. Conversations with passengers—ranging from wealthy professionals to struggling laborers—gave him insight into the city's evolving problems. Whether it was discussions about inflation, poor infrastructure, or political discontent, these interactions reinforced his understanding of people's frustrations and aspirations. Even as he worked long hours behind the wheel, Mama remained a political thinker, absorbing the pulse of the electorate through every ride.

As he became more adept at managing his finances, Mama realized that renting a taxi ate into his profits. Determined to own his vehicle, he secured a small loan, possibly from a cooperative bank or a trusted acquaintance. Purchasing his first taxi marked a turning point, though it came with the burden of repaying monthly installments. To clear his debts quickly, he adopted a disciplined approach—minimizing personal expenses, reinvesting profits, and ensuring timely loan payments. Once the first vehicle was fully paid off, he saved diligently and took calculated risks to purchase a second taxi. Over time, this pattern continued, allowing him to build a modest fleet of seven taxis. Each acquisition was a step toward financial security, giving him greater freedom to dedicate time to politics. Managing multiple taxis meant hiring trusted drivers, often acquaintances from the chawl who were struggling to find stable work. This arrangement ensured a steady income while allowing him to focus on his expanding political responsibilities.

Balancing his business with his political aspirations required immense discipline. Mornings were spent reviewing his taxi operations, addressing maintenance issues, and assigning routes to his drivers. By midday, his focus shifted to BJP activities—attending meetings, organizing rallies, and assisting constituents with civic issues. Evenings sometimes saw him back behind the wheel, picking up fares until midnight to ensure his financial stability. His taxi business was not just a source of income but an extension of his public work. Many of his passengers recognized him, and political discussions often arose naturally. Some sought his help with bureaucratic matters, while others expressed their views on governance. Word of his dual role as a taxi driver and political worker spread, and some passengers deliberately sought out his cab, intrigued by his unique journey. Through these interactions, Mama strengthened his image as a leader who remained connected to the common man.

Despite his growing influence, electoral success remained elusive. In the early 1980s, he contested another municipal election in Shivdi, a constituency known for its mix of industrial laborers, small traders, and long-time residents loyal to established parties. This time, the race was fiercely competitive, and Mama came heartbreakingly close to victory, losing by just 57 votes. The narrow margin was both encouraging and agonizing—it confirmed that he had built significant support, but it also underscored the challenges of breaking through entrenched political structures. His campaign, based on grassroots outreach and personal interactions, resonated with many, but his opponents had the advantage of financial resources and party machinery. The result was a bitter disappointment, yet it fueled his determination to refine his strategy, expand his reach, and prepare for future opportunities.

Even in defeat, Mama's reputation within the BJP continued to grow. Senior leaders recognized his dedication and rewarded him with greater organizational responsibilities. Under the guidance of Ram Naik, a prominent BJP figure, Mama was appointed Taluka Pramukh, overseeing party activities in his region. His role involved mobilizing volunteers, leading membership drives, and strengthening the party's grassroots presence. His effectiveness in this position earned him further elevation to District Deputy Head, where he became involved in broader policy discussions, election strategies, and community outreach programs. He became a key link between local citizens and party leadership, ensuring that real issues—such as housing concerns, labor rights, and infrastructure development—were addressed in political planning. His ability to mediate internal disputes and unify party workers made him an invaluable asset.

Mama's ability to balance multiple responsibilities—his taxi business, political duties, and community service—became a defining trait. His home became an informal office where residents sought assistance with various issues. Whether it was a family struggling with eviction, a small business owner navigating municipal regulations, or a young worker in need of career advice, Mama was always willing to help. His tireless work ethic inspired younger BJP volunteers, many of whom saw him as a mentor. Despite long hours and constant demands, he remained focused on his larger goal—serving the people and securing a leadership role where he could create real change.

His journey was marked by personal sacrifices. Family birthdays and quiet evenings at home were often interrupted by urgent political matters. Though he tried to make time for his wife and children, the demands of public life frequently pulled him away. However, his family understood that his work was driven by a deep sense of purpose. His children grew up watching him juggle responsibilities, learning valuable lessons about resilience, service, and the importance of standing up for one's beliefs.

Mama's willingness to learn from setbacks set him apart. Every election loss, every financial challenge, and every political struggle became a lesson. Rather than becoming discouraged, he used each experience to refine his approach. He worked on his public speaking skills, studied party manifestos, and built stronger networks within the community. His humility allowed him to accept feedback from both senior leaders and ordinary citizens, making him a more effective leader over time. Unlike many politicians who distanced themselves from the struggles of the poor, Mama remained deeply involved in ground realities. He knew that people cared less about ideological rhetoric and more about basic necessities—housing, water, employment, and education. His focus on practical solutions made him a trusted figure, even among those who traditionally supported rival parties.

Through perseverance and an unyielding commitment to service, Mama continued to strengthen his political standing. Though he had yet to win an election, his presence in the BJP was firmly established. His taxi years were more than just a phase of financial survival—they were a testament to his resilience, his ability to adapt, and his unwavering belief in the power of grassroots leadership. His story was not about immediate victories, but about long-term dedication, proving that leadership is built through years of consistent effort, rather than overnight success.

Despite another narrow election loss, Mama refused to retreat. He knew he was close, that with better planning and expanded outreach, he could one day secure the people's mandate. Meanwhile, his role within the BJP continued to grow, as senior leaders entrusted him with larger responsibilities. His journey from a taxi driver to a respected political organizer showed that true leadership is not about titles, but about action. His years behind the wheel shaped him into a leader who listened, understood, and never gave up—qualities that would one day propel him to even greater heights.

CHAPTER FOURTEEN

JOURNEY TO GANGAKHED (PARBHANI)

Sitaram "Mama" Ghandat's political journey had always been marked by perseverance and an unwavering commitment to the people. Until the mid-1980s, his political work was rooted in Mumbai, where he built his reputation as a dedicated worker in the Jan Sangh and later the Bharatiya Janata Party (BJP). But fate had something entirely unexpected in store for him. In what would become one of the most pivotal moments of his life, Mama was introduced to Gangakhed, a reserved constituency in Parbhani district, where he had no prior connections, no family ties, and no political foothold. Yet, within a few years, he transformed from a complete outsider into one of the region's most respected leaders.

Mama's introduction to Gangakhed was not something he had planned. It was the vision and insistence of two senior BJP leaders, Vasantrao Bhagwat and Uttamrao Patil, that set this journey into motion. Bhagwat, a selfless and respected figure in the party, saw something in Mama that convinced him this was the right man to lead the BJP in Gangakhed. Patil, a political mentor to many, treated Mama like a son and encouraged him to take on this challenge. They both recognized that the BJP needed strong leadership in

SC-reserved constituencies, and they believed that Mama's background—his personal struggles, grassroots activism, and deep connection with working-class people—made him the ideal candidate.

Initially, Mama hesitated. He had spent his entire life in Mumbai, and despite his extensive political work, he had never even visited his own native district of Ahmednagar or his Taluka, Parner. Now, he was being asked to relocate to a place where he had no roots. It was an enormous leap, one that carried great risk. But Bhagwat and Patil assured him that the people of Gangakhed needed a leader like him—someone who understood their hardships and would not abandon them after elections.

With their guidance, Mama took a decisive step. He gathered 8–10 jeeps, loaded them with BJP-Sena flags, and set out for Gangakhed within 24 hours. His first stop was Parali, where he met Gopinath Munde, a rising star in the BJP. Munde had a deep understanding of Marathwada politics and was instrumental in strengthening the party's presence in rural Maharashtra. He welcomed Mama and provided him with strategic guidance on how to approach Gangakhed. From there, Mama and his team proceeded to their final destination—a land completely unknown to them.

Upon arrival, the local BJP district head arranged for Mama's stay at the house of a respected businessman, Ram Babu Sarda. This temporary base became crucial for planning his movements across the constituency. Every morning, before sunrise, Mama set out in a vehicle to visit remote mountain villages, introducing himself to people who had never heard his name. Unlike seasoned politicians who often relied on mass rallies, Mama's approach was deeply personal. He sat with villagers in their homes, joined them in tea stalls, and listened to their concerns without making grand promises.

Despite his tireless efforts, he faced fierce resistance. The opposition, particularly four-time MLA Dynanoba Gaikwad, began spreading the narrative that Mama was an outsider from Mumbai with no real stake in Gangakhed's future. It was a potent argument in a rural setting, where local identity and long-standing relationships played a crucial role in elections. Many villagers were skeptical—why should they trust someone who had never lived in their region? What guarantee was there that he would not disappear after the elections?

Mama did not shy away from these accusations. Instead of pretending to be a long-time resident, he acknowledged his background and focused on what truly mattered—shared struggles. He spoke of his childhood poverty, of working as a cobbler and driving taxis to survive. He told them that while he may not have been born in Gangakhed, he understood their pain because he had lived through similar hardships. He reassured them that his commitment was not just for an election but for long-term change.

His work continued with relentless dedication. Even after losing the 1990 election despite securing the BJP ticket, he did not abandon Gangakhed. Vasantrao Bhagwat insisted that he stay and continue working with the people. Instead of retreating to Mumbai, Mama doubled down. He spent months, sometimes entire seasons, visiting every village, strengthening BJP's presence, and personally helping voters in whatever ways he could. He even took groups of villagers to Mumbai, introducing them to urban political dynamics and expanding their understanding of governance. Slowly but surely, he built a strong party organization where there had previously been none.

To counter the "outsider" label, Mama immersed himself in local life. He participated in village festivals, attended religious ceremonies, and even learned regional dialects to communicate more effectively. His strategy was simple—he would not just visit; he would stay. He would not just speak; he would listen. And he would not just promise; he would act.

His opponents relied on their established networks and financial resources, but Mama relied on something far more powerful—human connection. He made himself visible and accessible, ensuring that no village was left untouched. His commitment did not go unnoticed. Slowly, the skepticism began to fade. Villagers who had once dismissed him started seeing him as someone who genuinely cared. Women began discussing how Mama had helped resolve water issues, farmers started talking about his efforts to improve irrigation, and youth found inspiration in his perseverance.

The 1995 election marked a turning point. Against all odds, despite being relatively new to the region, Mama won. It was a victory not just for him but for every voter who had believed in his sincerity. It was proof that politics was not just about lineage or local connections—it was about showing up, working hard, and earning trust.

Mama's journey in Gangakhed was more than just a campaign; it was a testament to the power of persistence. He had entered as a stranger, faced resistance at every turn, and yet, through sheer determination, he had built something real. His story in Gangakhed is a reminder that leadership is not about where one comes from, but about where one chooses to stand. And Mama had chosen to stand with the people.

CHAPTER FIFTEEN

INDEPENDENT STAND

Between 1989 and 1995, Sitaram "Mama" Ghandat poured his heart into Gangakhed, a rural constituency in Parbhani district that had become his second home. After years of relentless travel, personal outreach, and grassroots organizing, he had built a deep connection with villagers who had once viewed him as an outsider from Mumbai. He had become a face of hope for many families longing for better roads, reliable water, and genuine representation in an SC-reserved constituency haunted by broken promises. Yet, just when he expected to reap the rewards of his work in the form of a BJP ticket for the 1995 elections, senior party leaders denied him the chance. Feeling deep disappointment and frustration, Mama embarked on an extraordinary path—he contested independently, propelled by his unwavering commitment to the people of Gangakhed.

Mama had spent years solidifying his presence in Gangakhed, making repeated visits to remote hamlets, listening to grievances, and slowly building a dedicated BJP cadre that believed in his sincerity. Unlike traditional politicians who appeared only during election seasons, he had made himself a constant presence, ensuring that people saw him not as a guest but as one of their own. His approach was simple—he did not just campaign; he lived the struggles of the people. He practically lived on the dusty roads of

Gangakhed, forming close relationships with farmers, shopkeepers, and laborers. He understood that winning trust was not about making promises but about showing up, time and again, when people needed help. During off-season months, when political activity slowed, he organized workshops on irrigation techniques, water conservation, and government schemes. Even when the ruling government was unsympathetic to BJP proposals, Mama's presence gave people hope—hope that someone was listening even when there were no votes at stake.

As an SC-reserved constituency, caste-based struggles played a major role in Gangakhed's daily life. Mama's own background helped him relate to these experiences, but he did not rely on identity alone to gain trust. He recognized that each sub-caste had unique concerns—some worried about educational neglect, others about land rights or economic marginalization. Rather than offering symbolic gestures or empty rhetoric, Mama engaged in deep conversations about empowerment. He spoke to students about higher education, encouraged farmers to form cooperatives, and worked with local groups to bridge divides within the SC community. Over time, he transcended the role of a political hopeful—he became a mentor, a problem solver, and a voice for those who had long felt ignored.

By the early 1990s, Mama had become a respected figure in Gangakhed. He had contested elections, shaped public discourse, and maintained an active role in everything from religious festivals to local infrastructure projects. Within the BJP's Parbhani district unit, he emerged as the de facto leader for the region. Senior BJP figures recognized his success in breaking into a constituency dominated by dynastic politics. More importantly, he had done it without massive financial backing, relying on outreach and genuine human connections. Yet, Mama knew that no matter how much trust he had built, the real test would come in the next election cycle. If he could secure the BJP nomination for a state assembly seat, all his years of effort could finally translate into real legislative power. He had laid the groundwork, but now he had to prove that his growing influence could turn into electoral victory.

As the 1995 Maharashtra state assembly elections approached, Mama believed he had earned the BJP ticket for Gangakhed. For six years, he had built trust, organized local committees, and expanded the party's base in an SC-reserved seat where the BJP had historically struggled. Few local workers disputed his claim—who else had done this level of groundwork? If anyone had a right to contest under the party banner, it was him. Yet, behind closed doors, tensions simmered. Rumors spread that BJP's higher leadership, particularly Pramod Mahajan and Gopinath Munde, were considering other candidates. Some party strategists argued that an older, more established figure with stronger financial backing or a recognizable political lineage might be a safer bet. Mama sensed unease among senior leaders, but rather than focusing on speculation, he intensified his efforts in Gangakhed to prove he was the people's choice.

Determined to fight for his rightful place, Mama began an intense period of lobbying, traveling to Mumbai and other key cities to meet BJP heavyweights. He sat face to face with Pramod Mahajan and Gopinath Munde, presenting letters of endorsement from Gangakhed's village heads, membership figures, and testimonies from residents who saw him as their only hope. His pitch was direct and impassioned—he had spent six years building the constituency for the party, and the people trusted him. He asked the leadership to recognize his work and grant him the nomination. Mahajan and Munde acknowledged his dedication, nodding at his efforts, but their responses remained vague. They spoke of party strategy, electoral calculations, and the bigger picture. Mama left the meetings with gnawing uncertainty—did they truly value his grassroots success, or were they more concerned with political deal-making?

In a final attempt to secure the nomination, Uttamrao Patil, who had mentored Mama and believed in his leadership, handed him a note to deliver directly to Munde. The message was clear—if given the ticket, Mama would win 100 percent. Patil's unwavering confidence in him was a testament to the years of work he had invested. But despite this endorsement, Mahajan and Munde refused to budge. The official BJP ticket went to another candidate.

The news devastated Mama, but he was not one to accept defeat easily. He could not walk away. He had a duty to prove that his connection with the constituency was stronger than any party affiliation.

With no party financial backing, Mama's campaign relied entirely on volunteer-driven, grassroots efforts. Farmers offered bullock carts for election tours, shopkeepers provided food and lodging, and young volunteers hand-painted posters. His campaign wasn't about grand rallies or elaborate speeches—it was about personal connections, built over years of genuine service. He was no longer a candidate; he was the people's choice.

As election day approached, Gangakhed braced for a showdown. Mama had defied the BJP, chosen the people over party loyalty, and now, the ballots would decide if his gamble would pay off. In an extraordinary turn of events, he emerged victorious. Against all odds, without the backing of a major party, he had won as an independent. His victory was not just a personal triumph—it was a powerful statement that political loyalty should always belong to the people, not to party elites.

Mama's victory in 1995 reshaped the political landscape of Gangakhed. He had proven that grassroots politics could triumph over party machinations, and his success became a beacon of hope for leaders who prioritized public service over political favoritism. From that moment onward, his relationship with Gangakhed was unbreakable. He had arrived as an outsider, fought against entrenched political interests, and emerged as a leader chosen by the people. This win marked the true beginning of his legacy—one built not on party allegiance, but on relentless dedication to the people he had sworn to serve.

CHAPTER SIXTEEN

VICTORY IN 1995: BIRTH OF THE 'INDEPENDENT MLA'

Throughout early 1995, Sitaram "Mama" Ghandat braced himself for an uphill battle in the Gangakhed constituency of Parbhani. Denied the BJP ticket despite years of grassroots work, he chose to run as an independent candidate—a daring leap that defied both conventional wisdom and party hierarchy. Many saw the decision as political suicide. Without deep financial resources or a prominent party symbol, how could one man overcome established contenders backed by major parties? Yet, on the day votes were tallied, Mama stunned the region by winning the Gangakhed seat by 476 votes, edging out heavyweight rivals and announcing himself as an unexpected force in Maharashtra's political landscape.

Mama's 1995 campaign was unlike any other. Running as an independent in a high-stakes election, he faced off against well-resourced candidates backed by major parties. Yet his bond with Gangakhed's rural population—cemented through personal visits, small-scale assistance, and trust built over years—fueled an electrifying grassroots movement that defied standard calculations. Lacking an official party banner, Mama relied on donations and help from villagers who believed in his sincerity. Scores of local volunteers stenciled homemade posters, used bullock carts to carry campaign materials, and guided him through remote hamlets where no other candidate bothered to go. His campaign stops were intimate gatherings under banyan trees or in open courtyards, where he reaffirmed his vow to stand by constituents even if that meant defying powerful party bosses. Each speech resonated with an authenticity voters craved in a district rife with cynicism about politics.

Because he was an independent, Mama did not rely on generic slogans or a pre-packaged manifesto. Instead, he spelled out core promises tailored to Gangakhed's immediate needs—better roads for sugarcane transport, reliable electricity for water pumps, and improved healthcare facilities. By focusing on bread-and-butter local issues, he struck a chord that soared above typical party-based rhetoric. The narrative was not about voting for a party symbol but about voting for Mama, the man who had already served them. Privately, he recognized that going independent entailed huge risks. Without the backing of a recognized party symbol or significant funding, he might face voter confusion or intimidation by bigger campaign machines. Despite these odds, every conversation with local supporters reaffirmed his decision. Village elders repeated a common refrain: "We don't care about party labels now. We want the person who stood by us."

As the election approached, an electric sense of possibility pervaded the constituency. Word spread of the unstoppable "Mama wave," fueled by a unique fusion of empathy, direct involvement, and local identity. By the final stretch, rival candidates took notice, scrambling to match Mama's personal rapport but largely failing to replicate its depth. When polling stations closed and ballots were counted, the entire district braced for a close outcome. Yet few anticipated just how close it would be—or which candidate would emerge on top. Late into the night, as boxes were opened and tallies updated, news leaked that Mama was leading in several critical pockets. In rural areas, counting often happened in a central facility, with supporters anxiously awaiting each round's results.

Mama's team huddled in a corner, exhausted but clinging to hope. Rival campaigners hovered about, some ridiculing the notion that an independent could win, while others eyed Mama's partial leads with growing unease.

In the early hours of the next morning, an election official declared the final margin—Mama had won by 476 votes. Jubilation erupted among his volunteers. Tears, hugs, and celebratory shouts echoed through the streets. The upset was monumental. Established candidates, backed by robust war chests and official party networks, found themselves dethroned by a man who had defied not just them but even the BJP's high command. At that moment, Gangakhed pivoted on its axis, rewriting local political assumptions. Mama's victory rippled beyond Parbhani. Journalists and political observers labeled him a "giant killer," praising his grassroots grit. Whispers spread through political circles that if one man's direct engagement could topple party machinery here, it could happen elsewhere too. Some in the BJP quietly regretted denying Mama the official ticket, while others insisted that his independent success validated the party's broader ideology of grassroots empowerment—ironically, since he had won outside their structure.

For Mama, the narrow margin represented the culmination of years of immersion in Gangakhed's villages. As he stood on a makeshift victory platform, addressing supporters who had rallied under a banner with no party symbol, his voice choked with emotion. "This is our triumph," he insisted, "yours and mine—proof that we don't need big parties to bring change." In politics, success often lures new allies. Hardly had Mama's victory sunk in when he received calls from various quarters—including the same BJP leaders who had refused him a ticket. They recognized Mama's valuable position as a newly minted MLA who commanded respect in a crucial constituency. Some BJP officials floated the idea that Mama could return to the party fold in the state assembly. They contended that, in legislative affairs, collaboration would benefit both Mama and the BJP's agenda.

Mama was torn. On one hand, he still subscribed to many BJP principles and had friends in that circle. On the other hand, the party leadership's denial remained a fresh wound. Accepting their overtures might signal that he was compromising the independent spirit that got him elected. Ultimately, Mama leaned on the voice of his constituents, who reminded him that he had won as an independent precisely because the BJP had spurned him. More strikingly, Mama began receiving signals from Bal Thackeray, the founder and supremo of Shiv Sena. Thackeray, known for his charismatic influence, saw Mama's victory as a potential synergy point for expanding Shiv Sena's influence in Marathwada. Mama found Bal Thackeray's sincerity appealing. After informal discussions, Mama declared his decision to associate more closely with Shiv Sena rather than returning to the BJP. This move raised eyebrows but also resonated with Mama's independent streak. He wanted alliances that respected his local commitments without overshadowing him.

One of the most remarkable moments in Mama's post-win trajectory came when Bal Thackeray offered him a ministerial position. For many politicians, a cabinet portfolio is the pinnacle of ambition—a ticket to power and influence. Yet Mama famously declined. Thackeray's invitation reportedly took place in a casual setting, where he praised Mama's grassroots commitment and suggested he take on a ministerial role. Mama, however, reflected on his limited formal education and felt that a legislative role better suited his strengths. He respectfully declined, explaining that while he honored Thackeray's trust, he did not want to embarrass the government or himself by struggling with complex policy matters. Instead, he preferred to focus entirely on constituency development. News of this refusal spread, reinforcing Mama's image as a leader uninterested in personal gain.

Having defied big-party structures and relinquished a ministerial post, Mama focused all his efforts on Gangakhed's pressing issues. He meticulously allocated his MLA development fund to road repairs, water supply schemes, school expansions, and small health center upgrades. Each project was selected based on direct input from local committees. Understanding the struggles of farmers, he encouraged cooperative farming models, revolving credit schemes, and self-help groups to reduce reliance on exploitative moneylenders. Even as an MLA, Mama did not retreat behind an official desk. He remained on the ground, personally overseeing infrastructure projects and resolving local disputes. Despite colleagues teasing him about rejecting comfortable government housing or luxury cars, he continued living simply, channeling resources into public welfare.

Mama's dramatic 1995 victory in Gangakhed marked the birth of a new kind of MLA in Maharashtra's political landscape. Defying the major parties, he ran on a shoestring budget, relying entirely on the trust of rural families. His triumph stunned seasoned politicians and proved that direct engagement could eclipse expensive campaigns. Offers from BJP leaders who had once dismissed him, and invitations from Bal Thackeray, revealed how power structures scrambled to align with his unstoppable momentum. Mama's decision to reject a ministerial position highlighted his deep sense of responsibility to his constituents. In the end, his victory was not just about winning an election but about redefining leadership—placing people above party lines and personal ambition. Gangakhed had become the stage for an underdog story that validated the power of grassroots democracy. Mama's next challenge would be proving that an independent MLA could govern as effectively as those backed by powerful party machines.

CHAPTER SEVENTEEN

TRANSFORMING GANGAKHED: FIRST TERM ACHIEVEMENTS

After defeating major party candidates in the 1995 elections and winning the Gangakhed seat as an independent, Sitaram "Mama" Ghandat entered the Maharashtra Legislative Assembly with something many politicians never achieve—a near-unbreakable trust from the people he represented. Determined to translate this trust into tangible results, Mama viewed his first term not as a time to bask in glory but as an opportunity to reform a constituency long ignored by mainstream powers. With a razor-thin victory margin of 476 votes, he felt compelled to prove that a people-centered approach could outperform large-party machines. His focus was clear—every action taken as an MLA had to directly improve the lives of his constituents.

Upon assuming office, Mama quickly identified the fundamental issues plaguing Gangakhed. The region suffered from woefully inadequate infrastructure, with poor roads, weak bridges, and patchy electricity that hindered both daily life and economic progress. Unlike past politicians who made empty promises, Mama moved quickly to bring development. He prioritized the construction and repair of rural roads to help farmers transport sugarcane, millet, and cotton to markets without being stalled by muddy, impassable routes during monsoons. Using the MLA development fund, supplemented by additional state grants, he initiated a wave of road projects, personally overseeing their progress to ensure accountability. The difference was quickly felt, as villagers no longer struggled to move their produce, and local businesses saw an increase in trade due to improved connectivity.

Recognizing that Gangakhed's geography presented major challenges in mobility, Mama also focused on building small but crucial bridges over the Godavari River. The lack of reliable crossings had long hindered travel, particularly for remote villages. By securing state funding and ensuring that contractors did not cut corners, Mama helped construct bridges that significantly reduced travel distances, allowing students to reach schools more easily and enabling farmers to transport perishable goods without delays. At the same time, he worked tirelessly to extend electricity to unconnected villages, bringing in new transformers and laying distribution lines to ensure stable power. This effort transformed night-time security, allowed for irrigation pump installations, and created opportunities for students to study in the evenings. Although bureaucratic red tape delayed some projects, Mama's constant follow-up ensured that the work progressed steadily.

Beyond infrastructure, Mama believed that education—especially for girls—was the key to breaking the cycle of poverty. Throughout his first term, he made school construction and accessibility a priority, overseeing the establishment or upgrade of 46 schools across Gangakhed. Some schools were built from scratch, while others were renovated to provide better facilities, including proper seating, ventilation, and toilets—crucial for older girls' attendance. Mama pressed education officials to appoint dedicated teachers, sometimes personally lobbying for vacant positions to be filled. His efforts bore fruit as more children, particularly girls, stayed in school, leading to a generational shift in attitudes toward education.

To further encourage female enrollment, Mama introduced small scholarships and free uniforms to ease financial burdens on families hesitant to send their daughters to school. He organized community outreach programs to convince parents that educating girls would improve their family's long-term prospects. Over time, the constituency saw a noticeable increase in female attendance, with young girls who might have been forced into early marriage instead continuing their studies. Mama's emphasis on higher education also led him to support students pursuing careers in engineering, medicine, and management. He helped top scorers secure scholarships, assisted with college admissions, and even traveled with students to major cities to navigate the complexities of higher education paperwork. For the first time, Gangakhed's youth saw professional careers as attainable goals, and the village celebrated every student who made it to a reputable college.

While infrastructure and education were central to his vision, Mama also focused on community welfare, ensuring fair distribution of resources and government aid. Unlike previous leaders who funneled benefits to loyal supporters, he insisted on transparent processes. He formed village-level committees to identify priority projects and ensure that development funds reached those who needed them most. Public meetings were held regularly to discuss government schemes, reducing the chances of corruption and favoritism. This approach not only streamlined development efforts but also built trust between the government and the people.

Mama also tackled financial challenges faced by marginal farmers and small traders. He worked with cooperative banks to introduce low-interest loans and microfinance programs, enabling entrepreneurs to start small businesses without falling into the trap of predatory moneylenders. His initiatives sparked a modest wave of rural entrepreneurship, with dairy farms, tailoring shops, and local trading businesses emerging as sustainable sources of income. On the health front, Mama organized free medical camps in remote villages, ensuring that residents received basic check-ups and treatment for common ailments. He pushed for improved sanitation and clean water access, particularly in SC-dominated settlements that had been historically neglected.

Understanding that social unity was essential for lasting development, Mama promoted communal harmony through inclusive celebrations and joint religious gatherings. His involvement in the immersion ceremony for Masaheb Meenatai Thackeray's ashes symbolized his alignment with Bal Thackeray and the broader Shiv Sena ideology while reinforcing his commitment to cultural respect and unity. The event saw thousands gather to pay tribute, strengthening ties between Gangakhed's diverse communities. Beyond large-scale functions, Mama frequently stepped in to mediate local disputes—whether between farmers over land rights or between religious groups over shared spaces. His ability to listen to all sides and find common ground earned him a reputation as a peacemaker.

As his first term progressed, the results of his efforts became undeniable. Gangakhed, once neglected, saw real improvements—better roads, electrification, and new schools transformed the landscape. Residents who had once doubted his independent candidacy now viewed him as the leader they had long hoped for. Word of his achievements spread beyond Gangakhed, drawing attention from political observers who marveled at how an independent MLA, operating without the backing of a major party, had managed to implement so many development projects. Some suggested that Mama's model—direct engagement with constituents, hands-on project management, and refusal to engage in corruption—could be replicated in other rural constituencies across Maharashtra.

Despite his successes, critics remained. Some accused Mama of favoring SC communities in his development plans, while others claimed his close ties with Shiv Sena limited his independence. Political opponents who had once dismissed him as an underdog now sought ways to undermine his growing influence. Yet, Mama remained unfazed, urging his detractors to visit the roads, schools, and villages transformed under his leadership before making judgments. He maintained that he was not interested in party politics but in delivering results for Gangakhed.

As his first term neared its end, speculation arose about whether he would run again. While he never took reelection for granted, his focus remained on the present—ensuring that his projects were completed, that no village was left behind, and that the trust placed in him was not misplaced. His message to the people was simple: let the work speak for itself. If the progress they had witnessed was meaningful, they would decide his future in the next election.

Mama's first term as an independent MLA was a testament to the power of grassroots leadership. By rejecting the traditional model of party-driven politics and staying close to his constituents, he proved that an independent representative could be just as effective—if not more so—than those backed by powerful political machines. His commitment to development over personal gain, his hands-on approach to problem-solving, and his refusal to engage in corruption set a new standard for governance in Gangakhed.

At the end of his first term, Gangakhed was no longer a forgotten constituency. It had become a symbol of what was possible when a leader put the people before politics. Mama's legacy was already taking shape—not as a politician who relied on party loyalty to win elections, but as a people's representative who had built his political career on trust, hard work, and an unyielding commitment to progress. His next challenge would be ensuring that this momentum was sustained in the years to come.

CHAPTER EIGHTEEN

SECOND TERM AS AN INDEPENDENT MLA

By the end of his first term in office, Sitaram "Mama" Ghandat had established himself as a steadfast proponent of grassroots development in Gangakhed. Few expected that the independent newcomer, who won by a narrow margin in 1995, could deliver so many concrete results—roads, schools, and a more equitable distribution of government resources. Yet his tangible achievements and direct style earned him an unexpectedly deep reservoir of public trust. When the 1999 elections approached, many believed Mama would face a formidable challenge from established parties eager to reclaim a seat lost to an "outsider." But Mama's second run not only secured his reelection, it solidified him as one of Gangakhed's most credible voices in the legislative arena.

When Mama first won Gangakhed as an independent candidate in 1995, many labeled his victory a fluke arising from popular anger at mainstream parties. By 1999, these skeptics expected a well-organized opposition—armed with party funds and influential endorsements—to oust him. But circumstances had changed. Mama now had a track record of major improvements, resonating strongly with local voters. Whereas his first campaign centered on authenticity and a personal bond with the people, the second had a powerful added dimension—results. Roads had been repaired, irrigation schemes were underway, and schools had expanded across Gangakhed. Mama no longer needed to rely on emotional appeals; he could point to tangible progress.

Much like four years earlier, Mama ran as an independent, though rumors circulated that multiple parties had tried to entice him with an official ticket. He remained committed to preserving his autonomy from high command dictates. His volunteer groups, now expanded with new supporters impressed by his first-term governance, organized corner meetings, distributed pamphlets summarizing Mama's achievements, and explained his vision for the next five years. Many of these gatherings took a celebratory tone, with families eager to share personal stories of how Mama's interventions had improved their daily lives. Across SC, OBC, and general communities, voters recognized that his policies had benefited all, undermining opponents' attempts to paint him as catering only to a specific section. Established local dynasties tried to rally support, but skepticism was widespread—where had these figures been when roads and schools were lacking?

On polling day, excitement lingered in the air, tempered by fears that mainstream parties would use financial muscle to manipulate votes. Yet when the results were declared, Mama not only won reelection, he did so by a stronger margin than in 1995. The victory proved that his success was no accident but rather an endorsement of his hands-on leadership. It confirmed that an independent MLA, when delivering results, could build sustained political credibility. Voters now saw themselves as active stakeholders in Mama's platform of local empowerment. Even his rivals acknowledged that dislodging him would require more than standard campaign theatrics.

Buoyed by this electoral validation, Mama entered his second term determined to scale up the projects he had started. While officially remaining an independent, the trust and respect he had earned translated into a level of local authority rarely seen in a single-constituency MLA. His leadership style remained grounded in direct interaction with people, continuing his village visits and ensuring constituents felt comfortable approaching him with their concerns. This on-the-ground presence kept him above petty politics, and even those who had not voted for him conceded that he was a genuine force for development.

With reelection came increased leverage in negotiating resources with government departments. Civil engineers, irrigation officials, and education commissioners had witnessed the effectiveness of his first-term projects, making them more receptive to his proposals. Where some had previously dismissed him as a temporary phenomenon, they now recognized his ability to mobilize local cooperation and complete projects efficiently. This credibility also led to the growth of civic engagement within Gangakhed. Youth forums, women's self-help groups, and farmers' collectives took inspiration from Mama's emphasis on self-reliance, forming their own planning committees to prioritize local needs. Mama encouraged these initiatives, shifting from being the sole decision-maker to a catalyst for local leadership.

Infrastructure remained a priority. Having upgraded village roads in his first term, Mama now focused on linking clusters of hamlets to state highways and market towns. These improvements boosted trade efficiency, reduced transportation costs, and enhanced bus connectivity. Farmers benefited from faster access to markets, and students no longer had to travel long distances on rough roads to reach schools. Recognizing Marathwada's perennial water shortages, Mama expanded irrigation initiatives, lobbying for minor irrigation dams and the deepening of existing water bodies. By securing government support for pipeline extensions, he helped remote areas access reliable water sources, mitigating the effects of recurring droughts.

Mama also continued his mission to improve educational infrastructure. With enrollment increasing from his previous efforts, he identified the need for expanded school capacity. He secured grants to add new classrooms, particularly in middle and high schools, ensuring students had facilities that supported their academic progress. His advocacy led to a surge in teacher appointments and training programs, ensuring that rural educators received updated pedagogical knowledge. Mama also strengthened scholarship programs for SC and marginalized students, working with local banks and donors to ensure financial support for college aspirants. Families that once viewed higher education as an unreachable goal now saw their children attending engineering, medical, and management institutions, marking a significant shift in Gangakhed's socio-economic landscape.

One of the defining features of Mama's second term was his pioneering approach to accountability. Frustrated by the lack of transparency in politics, he decided to document his achievements in a Work Report Book. This comprehensive record detailed every road built, school upgraded, and water scheme implemented under his tenure, including budget allocations and completion timelines. It was an unprecedented move in local governance, empowering constituents to track progress and verify claims. Mama publicly distributed copies at a community gathering, inviting scrutiny and encouraging people to hold him accountable. Supporters hailed it as a new standard in democratic transparency, while skeptics combed through it for discrepancies. Some political observers noted that the report could serve as a model for rural governance across Maharashtra.

Beyond development, Mama focused on social unity, positioning himself as a leader above caste and religious divides. He ensured that major projects had representation from all communities, promoting inclusive decision-making. Festivals became opportunities for cross-community interaction, fostering a spirit of cooperation rather than competition. His role in organizing interfaith celebrations and resolving local disputes reinforced his standing as a unifier. The symbolic immersion of Masaheb Meenatai Thackeray's ashes in the Godavari, an event Mama helped organize, blended his allegiance to Bal Thackeray with a broader message of cultural respect and unity.

As his second term progressed, Mama's influence extended beyond Gangakhed. Observers from neighboring districts and even state-level politicians took note of his governance model—an independent MLA delivering large-scale development without the backing of a major party. Some political figures sought to replicate elements of his approach, particularly his emphasis on direct engagement and transparency. However, rival parties also intensified efforts to challenge him in future elections, recognizing that his growing influence posed a long-term threat to established political structures.

Despite his successes, challenges remained. Large-scale water management solutions and advanced healthcare systems required state-level coordination beyond an independent MLA's reach. Job creation for educated youths returning from urban centers remained a concern. Some critics accused Mama of overreliance on his personal brand, warning that long-term progress required institutional frameworks beyond individual leadership. Mama acknowledged these realities, advocating for stronger state partnerships while emphasizing the need for local self-reliance.

As talk of the next election cycle began, speculation grew over whether Mama would run again. While he never took reelection for granted, his focus remained on ensuring that ongoing projects were completed and that local committees took ownership of development initiatives. His message to the people was clear: sustainable progress could not depend on one leader but required collective responsibility.

Mama's second term reinforced the idea that independent leadership, when grounded in genuine public service, could rival and even surpass party-backed governance. His work in infrastructure, education, and social unity transformed Gangakhed from a neglected region into a constituency recognized for its bottom-up development. The Work Report Book cemented his reputation for accountability, while his efforts to bridge caste and religious divisions strengthened the social fabric. As his term came to a close, Gangakhed stood as a testament to what was possible when governance was driven by trust, integrity, and an unwavering commitment to the people.

The question that now loomed was whether Mama's independent success could be sustained against mounting political pressures. Would Gangakhed's transformation continue, or would mainstream parties regain control? The next election would determine whether Mama's model of governance had reshaped the political landscape permanently or if traditional forces would reassert themselves.

CHAPTER NINETEEN

ABHYUDAYA BANK AND THE COOPERATIVE SECTOR

Even as Sitaram "Mama" Ghandat made his mark in electoral politics as an independent MLA in Gangakhed, he never abandoned his deep involvement in the cooperative movement. Decades before he rose to prominence in the legislative arena, Mama played a key role in Abhyudaya Bank, a cooperative institution that would become one of the largest in Maharashtra. His journey from a humble participant to a Director and eventually Chairman reflected a lifelong belief in using cooperative models to foster social and economic development. Parallel to this, Mama supported educational ventures under Abhyudaya's umbrella, guiding the growth of Abhyudaya Education High School, which became a pillar for thousands of students. His contributions to Abhyudaya Bank's expansion, the creation of employment opportunities, and his role in cooperative-led educational initiatives underscored his vision of inclusive progress.

Mama's association with Abhyudaya Bank dates back to the 1960s, well before he became a political figure. At the time,

Abhyudaya was a modest urban cooperative bank in Mumbai, catering to the financial needs of workers, small traders, and daily earners who found mainstream commercial banks intimidating or inaccessible. As a young man struggling for a stable livelihood while working as a cobbler and renting taxis, Mama found the cooperative model appealing. It offered small loans at fair rates and reinvested profits back into community services rather than paying dividends to distant shareholders. This people-centric approach resonated with Mama's empathy and down-to-earth style. He began as a simple member, appreciating how the bank extended microloans to marginalized individuals. Over time, he realized that by pooling community resources and managing them transparently, cooperatives could uplift entire neighborhoods.

Mama's natural ability to connect with ordinary members soon caught the attention of Abhyudaya's core management. He volunteered to help illiterate customers fill out forms, assisted daily-wage laborers with basic savings plans, and explained the benefits of cooperative banking to hesitant first-time depositors. By the late 1960s, he earned a reputation as a bridge between the bank and working-class clientele who found formal banking procedures daunting. Recognizing his sincerity, the board invited him to take on broader responsibilities, first as a committee member and later as a Director overseeing membership drives and small-branch operations. Even before he rose to political prominence, Mama championed clear communication, urging bank staff to treat each depositor with dignity and educate customers on financial literacy. His efforts encouraged many daily-wage workers, who had previously relied on informal savings methods, to trust Abhyudaya Bank as a reliable institution for securing their hard-earned money.

Mama's role in Abhyudaya grew over the years, culminating in his appointment as Chairman. At the time, the bank stood at a crossroads, with the potential for major growth if guided wisely. Under his leadership, alongside a dedicated board, Abhyudaya Bank embarked on an ambitious expansion strategy, growing from 16 to 111 branches across Mumbai, Maharashtra, and beyond. Mama and his colleagues believed that cooperative banking should extend beyond urban centers to semi-rural areas where private banks rarely ventured. By opening branches in smaller towns, Abhyudaya reached artisans, farmers, and small businesses in need of accessible finance. The bank's total business surged to approximately ₹17,000 crores, making it one of India's leading multi-state scheduled cooperative banks. Mama attributed this growth to the grassroots trust the bank nurtured, as many depositors were first-time savers assured by its community-driven ethos.

As Chairman, Mama pushed for transparent governance and accountability. Annual general meetings became open forums where members could voice concerns and review financial reports. Recognizing the importance of modernization, he advocated for computerized banking systems to curb manual errors and streamline transactions. Despite resistance from older staff, Mama ensured the adoption of ATM services and online banking, positioning Abhyudaya as a competitive cooperative institution. However, rapid expansion brought challenges, including the risk of mismanagement and bad loans. To counter these risks, Mama and the board instituted strict internal audits and emphasized staff training. Critics feared that the bank's rapid growth might dilute its cooperative spirit, but Mama ensured that each branch retained its localized, customer-first approach.

Beyond expanding Abhyudaya's footprint, Mama leveraged its success to uplift his constituency in Gangakhed, particularly by facilitating employment opportunities. Over time, Abhyudaya's growing network required skilled and semi-skilled staff, from tellers and accountants to branch managers and customer service representatives. Mama ensured that around 300 individuals from Gangakhed's SC and underprivileged communities secured fair opportunities at the bank. While all applicants had to meet eligibility criteria, Mama made certain that recruitment drives extended to Gangakhed, offering local youth a chance at stable employment. For many families, securing a job at Abhyudaya was transformative, providing financial security and upward mobility. Some of these employees climbed the ranks, managing branches and contributing to the bank's continued success.

Mama's influence extended beyond employment. Under his leadership, Abhyudaya expanded its presence into smaller towns, including areas near Gangakhed, where farmers and small traders had previously been reliant on moneylenders. With Abhyudaya's accessible loan options, farmers could secure funding for seeds and equipment without falling into debt traps. Mama's efforts also helped establish microloan schemes that enabled small entrepreneurs, including women's self-help groups, to launch home-based businesses. This alignment between cooperative banking and local economic upliftment reinforced the idea that financial self-reliance could be achieved through collective ownership rather than dependency on external aid.

Parallel to his banking initiatives, Mama was deeply involved in Abhyudaya Education High School, which served the children of mill workers and low-income families in Mumbai's Parel area. Recognizing the potential of education to break cycles of poverty, Mama guided the school's expansion, helping it grow to an institution that served over 7,000 students. The school provided quality education at affordable fees, ensuring that children from disadvantaged backgrounds had access to learning resources. Under Mama's influence, Abhyudaya High School developed well-equipped classrooms, libraries, and computer labs, while also emphasizing extracurricular activities to create a well-rounded learning environment. He played an active role in securing scholarships for financially struggling students and worked to ensure that graduates could transition into higher education or stable jobs.

Mama frequently attended school events, delivering motivational speeches that emphasized hard work, discipline, and the power of education to overcome caste and class barriers. Teachers recalled him as an approachable mentor who not only supported students but also advocated for teacher training programs and improved working conditions. His philosophy was simple: a well-supported teaching staff created a better learning experience for students. In many ways, the school mirrored the values of Abhyudaya Bank, reinforcing community-driven progress through transparency, inclusivity, and long-term planning.

Mama's experiences in the cooperative banking and education sectors shaped his broader approach to governance. He firmly believed that economic empowerment and education were intertwined, and he sought to replicate Abhyudaya's cooperative principles in his political work. By ensuring community participation in decision-making, maintaining financial transparency, and focusing on sustainable growth, he demonstrated that bottom-up development could be both effective and scalable. His legacy at Abhyudaya was not just in expanding its financial reach but in embedding a culture of trust, accessibility, and social responsibility.

By the time Mama stepped away from his role as Chairman, Abhyudaya Bank had evolved into a powerhouse institution, serving thousands across multiple states. His dual contributions to cooperative banking and education showcased how economic empowerment could be leveraged for lasting societal change. His commitment to financial inclusion, job creation, and accessible education reflected his broader mission to uplift marginalized communities through practical, people-centric solutions.

In the grand narrative of Mama's life, his leadership at Abhyudaya Bank and Abhyudaya Education High School stands as a testament to the power of cooperative models in driving large-scale transformation. By ensuring that financial and educational institutions remained anchored in community needs rather than profit motives, he demonstrated that true leadership is not about wielding authority but about fostering systems that empower ordinary people. His work left an enduring impact, proving that cooperative movements, when guided by integrity and social responsibility, can become engines of sustainable progress.

CHAPTER TWENTY

A BRIEF PAUSE AND THE 2004 SETBACK

By the early 2000s, Sitaram "Mama" Ghandat had served two consecutive independent terms in the Gangakhed constituency, solidifying his reputation as an empathetic, results-driven legislator. His focus on tangible development—improved roads, expanded educational infrastructure, and cooperative-based progress—had resonated deeply with voters. Yet politics is rarely linear. In 2004, Mama lost his seat, a development that shocked many observers who had grown accustomed to his consistent success. This unexpected electoral defeat forced him to reflect on the evolving political landscape, the impact of shifting constituency boundaries, and the nature of public service. Despite stepping away from formal office, Mama continued to nurture relationships in Gangakhed, staying engaged in social and cooperative initiatives that had long defined his leadership.

As the 2004 state assembly elections approached, Mama prepared to defend a constituency he had ably represented for nearly a decade. However, local dynamics and broader political currents had evolved significantly since his prior victories in 1995 and 1999. Gangakhed, which had once been designated as an SC-reserved seat, underwent a re-evaluation due to the Delimitation Commission's changes or standard adjustments following census reviews. These changes, which occasionally affected constituency boundaries and reservation statuses, had implications for electoral strategy. If Gangakhed was no longer SC-reserved, or if its geographical composition changed, it could attract fresh competitors backed by stronger political machinery. Even if the constituency remained SC-reserved, new challengers from similar backgrounds emerged with major party support, altering the political landscape in ways that Mama, as an independent, had to navigate.

Mama's repeated successes had not gone unnoticed by established political forces. While he had built his victories on grassroots support, major parties sought to reclaim the seat, viewing his independent status as a disruption to traditional power structures. Ahead of 2004, a concerted effort materialized to weaken his influence. Well-funded campaigns depicted him as politically isolated, with opponents suggesting that larger parties could bring more "modern" solutions to Gangakhed's issues. Meanwhile, Mama's grassroots network, which had been the backbone of his previous campaigns, faced new challenges. Many longtime volunteers struggled with financial and logistical constraints, making it harder to maintain the same energy and outreach as in past elections.

On election day, voter turnout was high, and many believed Mama could once again defy the odds. Yet the final count revealed a decisive loss. The defeat, though not by an overwhelming margin, was sufficient to end his tenure as MLA. Immediate reactions among constituents ranged from disbelief to sadness. Many families, who had only known Mama as their representative for a decade, struggled to process the outcome. Some questioned how a leader who had transformed infrastructure, improved irrigation, and expanded education could be replaced. For Mama, the loss was both a personal and political reckoning. While he had faced electoral defeats before, this one followed a period of sustained progress, forcing him to reassess the shifting political climate and his future role in public service.

The 2004 setback, though disappointing, did not diminish Mama's understanding of political cycles. He had experienced losses in earlier phases—particularly in municipal elections in Mumbai and near-misses in Gangakhed before his eventual victories. However, this defeat came after two successful terms, making it a moment for deep reflection. One factor was the changing nature of reserved and general seats. Over time, constituencies designated as SC-reserved can be reclassified as general seats, opening them to broader competition. Mama had built strong support across castes, but such reclassification inevitably altered electoral dynamics, sometimes activating caste-based voting patterns or attracting new, well-funded candidates. Regardless of these changes, Mama remained steadfast in his belief that leadership should transcend caste lines and be rooted in tangible development.

Beyond the technical aspects of seat reclassification, Mama also recognized that a decade in office could lead to voter fatigue. While his supporters remained loyal, some sections of the electorate may have sought a new face, regardless of past achievements. Mama acknowledged that years of continuous campaigning and governing had taken a toll on his grassroots movement. Without a formal party structure to shoulder the campaign burden, every reelection required immense personal effort. The 2004 campaign, despite its sincerity, may not have generated the same momentum as the mid-1990s races, where he was seen as a rising force. However, even as he processed the loss, Mama looked around Gangakhed and saw the roads, irrigation channels, schools, and community centers he had fought to create. These developments, he reminded supporters, would remain regardless of who held the MLA seat.

Rather than retreat from public life, Mama chose to stay engaged with the people of Gangakhed. While some advised him to step back and reassess before considering another electoral bid, he felt a responsibility to ensure that the progress made under his leadership was not reversed. He continued visiting villages, maintaining relationships with families who had come to rely on his guidance.

"You are still our Mama," many constituents told him, reinforcing that his leadership was about more than holding an official title. Village committees that he had helped establish—whether for road maintenance, small cooperative ventures, or microfinance initiatives—continued seeking his input. Though he no longer controlled MLA funds, he used his connections to facilitate access to government schemes, philanthropic donors, and cooperative resources.

Many infrastructural and educational projects launched during his tenure were still under construction at the time of his loss. Rather than abandon them, Mama worked behind the scenes to ensure they remained on track. He introduced the new MLA and local administrative heads to the scope of ongoing developments, urging them to prioritize continuity over political rivalry. Some initiatives faced bureaucratic hurdles, but Mama leveraged his credibility to keep them moving forward. Additionally, villagers still approached him for help with everyday governance issues—land disputes, ration card applications, and municipal approvals. His extensive experience allowed him to navigate government channels, even as an ex-MLA, ensuring that those who sought his assistance did not feel abandoned.

Despite his loss, Mama remained deeply involved in cooperative and social initiatives. He continued his leadership roles in Abhyudaya Bank and educational organizations, ensuring that financial and educational empowerment remained accessible to his constituents. Some critics speculated whether he would align with a major party for a future election, but Mama maintained that his commitment was to Gangakhed first, not political affiliations. He remained open to strategic alliances but refused to compromise on the independent, people-centric approach that had defined his career.

The political landscape in Gangakhed inevitably shifted with Mama's departure from office. The new MLA, backed by a major party, sought to establish their own identity. Some attempts were made to diminish Mama's contributions—renaming projects or claiming credit for developments initiated during his tenure. However, these efforts were met with skepticism. Villagers, who had directly benefited from Mama's leadership, continued to reference him when discussing ongoing community needs. While rival parties attempted to consolidate power, Mama's continued presence in the constituency ensured that his legacy was not easily erased.

For Mama, the 2004 election loss was a humbling moment but not a defeat in the larger sense. He took the time to reflect, recognizing that leadership was not defined by continuous electoral victories but by the ability to create lasting impact. While some encouraged him to prepare for a return to politics in 2009, he remained patient, believing that the people of Gangakhed would decide when and if they needed him again. In the meantime, he remained committed to community work, strengthening cooperative models, and ensuring that the principles of self-reliance and development continued to shape Gangakhed's progress.

As time passed, Mama's influence remained visible in the roads that connected villages, the schools that provided education to thousands, and the cooperative networks that sustained local businesses. His approach to leadership, centered on trust and transparency, endured even outside formal political office. While the 2004 loss marked a brief pause in his electoral career, it did not signal the end of his journey. Instead, it reinforced the idea that true leadership is measured not by the length of time in office but by the depth of one's impact on the lives of ordinary people. Whether or not he would return to the political arena remained uncertain, but his continued engagement in Gangakhed ensured that his vision for the constituency remained alive.

CHAPTER TWENTY-ONE

RESURGENCE IN 2009: THIRD TERM WIN

After losing the Gangakhed seat in 2004, many observers assumed that Sitaram "Mama" Ghandat's remarkable run as an independent MLA had reached its natural conclusion. He had held the constituency for two successful terms—first in 1995, then in 1999—and even though his people-centered style had left a deep imprint on Gangakhed, political currents in the 2004 election had temporarily turned against him. Yet, Mama remained active in cooperative ventures, community outreach, and behind-the-scenes guidance in the region. Five years later, a striking opportunity emerged when the Gangakhed seat was reclassified as a general constituency rather than SC-reserved, reopening the field to a broader array of candidates. Against the backdrop of shifting electoral alliances and well-funded opposition, Mama mounted a comeback that stunned many, winning by a margin of 16,000 votes over heavyweight opponents, including a sitting state minister and a prominent BJP figure. This victory showcased how he shattered caste boundaries and overcame the financial muscle of mainstream campaigns to reclaim the seat he once called home.

Since the mid-1990s, Gangakhed had held SC-reserved status, ensuring representation for historically marginalized communities. However, seat reservations undergo periodic revisions based on population shifts and legal frameworks. By 2009, Gangakhed underwent boundary adjustments, changing from an SC-reserved seat to a general seat open to candidates from any caste background. This shift drastically widened the electoral field, attracting established parties that had previously avoided the seat due to a lack of strong SC leadership. For Mama, this change posed both an opportunity and a risk. While he had long demonstrated an ability to transcend caste lines even in an SC seat, the removal of that reservation meant he would face a broader range of rivals, including influential local figures and big-party candidates with deep financial backing. After his 2004 loss, Mama had focused on cooperative development, educational projects, and maintaining his grassroots ties in Gangakhed. Constituents urged him to contest again, arguing that his track record spoke volumes regardless of the seat's caste classification. Though he appreciated the break from legislative duties, he never stopped caring about the district's progress. If voters truly wanted him back, he felt obliged to step in and challenge powerful parties once more. Staying true to his independent approach, Mama decided not to align himself with a mainstream party that might hinder his people-first ideology. Despite receiving offers from multiple groups, he reaffirmed his independent stance, relying on the trust he had built over decades.

The 2009 election posed a major challenge, with two formidable opponents standing in Mama's way: a sitting state minister from one of the ruling parties and a well-backed BJP candidate with statewide recognition. Many presumed that Mama, running without a major party symbol, would be overshadowed by these well-funded figures. The state minister possessed not only the full weight of his office but also the resources of a major party, leveraging government programs to attract voter allegiance. Local leaders expected him to overpower Mama's grassroots style, yet voters quietly recalled Mama's sincerity in completing roads, water lines, and school expansions. Meanwhile, the BJP, determined to reclaim seats across Marathwada, fielded a well-known candidate who had contested or held offices in other regions. With strong party machinery and national-level strategies, he aimed to attract rural votes by offering modern solutions and party-backed policies. Mama, now an independent candidate, faced the possibility of his former BJP allies working against him, similar to the 1995 friction. Despite the stacked odds, Mama's campaign strategy remained unchanged. He relied on personal interactions, minimal but impactful posters, and repeated visits to every corner of Gangakhed. Unlike his opponents, who held large rallies and distributed promotional materials, Mama focused on smaller gatherings where he could listen directly to people's concerns. His campaign relied heavily on village committees that took ownership of distributing leaflets highlighting his past achievements and his vision for the future. Many of Mama's longtime supporters rejoined the campaign, recalling how he never truly abandoned them even when out of office. They championed him as the people's candidate, unaffiliated with party power plays.

On election day, the tension was palpable. Early tallies showed a tight race, but as more votes were counted, Mama's lead expanded significantly. By the final count, he had won by a commanding margin of over 16,000 votes, a significantly larger gap than his earlier victories. This victory sent shockwaves through the political landscape, silencing critics who had dismissed him after his 2004 loss. His overwhelming margin proved that years of continuous grassroots presence had paid off, eliminating doubts that his previous wins were flukes. The scale of Mama's victory over a sitting state minister demonstrated voters' trust in his track record over election-season promises. The BJP candidate, despite having the backing of a national party, also fell short, with many voters believing Mama's work in Gangakhed spoke louder than campaign rhetoric. Perhaps most significantly, Mama's win occurred in a general seat, free of SC-reservation constraints. He secured votes from across caste lines, reinforcing his reputation as an inclusive leader who prioritized development over identity politics. Upper-caste farmers, small business owners, and religious minorities comfortably supported him, trusting his sincerity and commitment to local progress. Celebrations erupted across Gangakhed as villagers rejoiced in Mama's return. Drummers and dancers filled the streets, families invoked blessings, and community feasts were organized. Mama, however, remained humble, reminding supporters that the real work lay ahead in sustaining and expanding progress across the constituency.

The significance of the 2009 victory extended beyond reclaiming the MLA seat. It proved the durability of Mama's leadership, demonstrating that independent candidates could thrive if they maintained genuine relationships and delivered results. His return showed that losing an election did not equate to losing public trust. His victory also reinforced the importance of grassroots politics over financial muscle. Despite running against well-funded party candidates, Mama's simple yet effective strategy of direct engagement proved that authentic connections with constituents outweighed campaign extravagance. His win also had implications for state politics, with analysts recognizing that the "Mama brand" had grown stronger, not weaker, during his five-year absence. Other grassroots politicians began emulating his hands-on style, while major parties privately assessed how to counter his independent model in future elections. For Gangakhed, Mama's return was a sign that local governance would once again prioritize transparency, accountability, and visible progress.

Emerging from his victory, Mama carried the weight of renewed expectations. He set clear goals for reengaging with past projects that had stalled under the previous MLA. Road expansions, irrigation channels, and education reforms were among his first priorities. With Gangakhed's new general constituency status, he also worked to integrate newly added wards and ensure balanced development across all communities. Reflecting on his five-year gap, Mama saw the period as a learning experience that had allowed him to identify deeper systemic challenges and explore innovative solutions through cooperative networks. He frequently reminded supporters that no MLA seat is permanent and that elected representatives must continuously evolve to meet people's needs. Rather than viewing his win as an entitlement, he saw it as a renewed mandate to serve with greater accountability. His focus on community-driven development remained steadfast, ensuring that Gangakhed would benefit from sustained growth rather than temporary campaign pledges.

Mama's third-term victory in 2009 stood as one of the most compelling chapters in his political career. Winning a general seat by a substantial margin disproved the notion that his past success depended solely on SC-reservation dynamics. His ability to defeat a sitting state minister and a well-supported BJP figure reaffirmed that direct community engagement and proven development work outweighed financial and party backing. This resurgence validated the cyclical nature of democracy, where voters ultimately prioritize results over party allegiance. With his return, Gangakhed was poised for another wave of developmental initiatives under Mama's hallmark governance style, emphasizing rigorous accountability, grassroots committees, and a relentless focus on improving everyday lives. His 2009 triumph was more than a political comeback; it was a testament to how sustained, people-oriented leadership could persist despite shifting electoral landscapes and powerful opposition.

CHAPTER TWENTY-TWO

FURTHER DEVELOPMENTAL MILESTONES

By the time Sitaram "Mama" Ghandat secured his third term in 2009—winning the Gangakhed seat as an independent in a now general constituency—he had already reshaped much of the region's infrastructure and social services. Over the following years, Mama used his revitalized mandate to intensify large-scale development projects, from water schemes and electricity distribution to public welfare programs and community-building initiatives. His unwavering focus on local empowerment translated into more robust irrigation networks, major cooperative-driven progress, free group weddings, expanded healthcare, and the systematic use of MLA funds to strengthen village infrastructure.

Gangakhed's semi-arid landscape and frequent water shortages had always compelled Mama to champion reliable irrigation and electricity. After his return in 2009, he scaled up these efforts, recognizing that fully integrated water supply and power distribution networks were key to helping farmers and small enterprises thrive. His plan involved utilizing the Godavari River for large-scale water-lift schemes to carry water to elevated farmlands, reducing farmers' reliance on erratic rainfall. He worked closely with irrigation officials to ensure these projects were executed without bureaucratic delays. To address drinking-water scarcity, he spearheaded multi-village pipeline projects that connected remote hamlets to central water reservoirs, delivering potable water directly to households. These projects were managed by trained village committees responsible for maintenance, ensuring sustainability. At the same time, he encouraged micro-irrigation methods such as drip irrigation and sprinkler systems, which significantly improved water efficiency. By providing subsidies and technical support, he helped farmers transition from wasteful irrigation techniques to modern, sustainable practices.

Electricity distribution was another area where Mama made a lasting impact. While his previous efforts had brought basic electrification to villages, unreliable voltage and overburdened transformers often led to disruptions. He pushed for the establishment of 33 kV sub-centers to improve power supply for agricultural and household use. These sub-centers ensured more stable electricity, especially for irrigation pumps, which in turn improved crop yields and reduced farming expenses. Recognizing that outdated transformers were a common cause of voltage drops, he worked with Maharashtra's power distribution company to replace inefficient transformers and install additional units to manage the growing demand. Mama also focused on preventing electricity theft, which was a significant issue in some areas. Through public awareness campaigns, he educated people on how unauthorized tapping led to power shortages, encouraging local vigilance to curb illegal usage. His initiatives also extended to supporting small businesses and local industries by advocating for dedicated power feeders that provided uninterrupted electricity to small-scale entrepreneurs, allowing local commerce to flourish.

Beyond infrastructure, Mama focused heavily on cooperative-driven solutions to strengthen Gangakhed's economy. He continued to push for major irrigation projects, rehabilitating older canals and constructing new links that provided more consistent water supply to farmland. He expanded watershed programs, ensuring that tanks and check dams were built in strategic locations to retain rainwater and recharge groundwater levels. These efforts minimized the impact of weak monsoons and improved the overall agricultural output. His vision for farmer empowerment extended beyond irrigation; he actively encouraged the formation of crop procurement cooperatives, which allowed farmers to collectively negotiate better prices for their produce and avoid middlemen exploitation. Many of these cooperatives also included storage facilities, enabling farmers to store grains and wait for market conditions to improve before selling their produce. He also advocated for fair crop pricing and worked on improving insurance schemes, ensuring that farmers had a financial safety net in case of natural calamities.

Mama's third term also saw significant social welfare initiatives aimed at reducing economic burdens on marginalized families. One of the most impactful programs was his introduction of free group weddings for financially struggling couples. Understanding that wedding expenses often led to crippling debt for low-income families, Mama organized mass marriage ceremonies where multiple couples could marry with dignity at no cost. These events, funded through a combination of MLA funds, cooperative contributions, and local donations, provided couples with wedding attire, rituals, and a communal feast. These ceremonies not only alleviated financial stress but also reinforced social unity by encouraging inter-community participation. Additionally, he allocated portions of the MLA fund to provide small grants for orphans and elderly citizens with no financial support, ensuring that those in the most vulnerable positions received at least basic assistance.

Mama also spearheaded critical improvements in healthcare infrastructure. Recognizing that many Primary Health Centers lacked basic facilities, he worked to upgrade them with better medical equipment, additional wards, and regular staffing to ensure consistent healthcare delivery. His efforts extended to establishing a rural hospital with minor surgical capabilities, reducing the need for patients to travel to distant cities for treatment. Mobile medical units were introduced to serve remote villages, providing vaccinations, screenings, and basic treatments for common ailments. In addition to physical healthcare improvements, he emphasized preventive healthcare awareness, encouraging families to adopt better hygiene and nutritional habits to reduce the incidence of preventable diseases.

Throughout his third term, Mama maintained his signature approach to governance—ensuring that every project was community-driven and financially transparent. He strategically allocated MLA development funds to build and renovate community centers, libraries, and cultural spaces, which became hubs for civic engagement and educational activities. His infrastructure initiatives extended to constructing drainage systems, village bus stands, and improved street lighting in rural areas. Unlike many politicians who viewed MLA funds as an entitlement, Mama treated them as an investment in long-term community development, ensuring that each project had a clear purpose and measurable impact. To maintain public trust, he regularly published reports on fund allocation and encouraged local oversight committees to monitor progress.

By integrating large-scale infrastructure projects with cooperative models and targeted welfare programs, Mama created a holistic development framework that empowered communities at every level. His irrigation and electricity initiatives directly boosted agricultural productivity, his cooperative programs gave farmers greater economic stability, and his welfare schemes reduced financial strain on families. Mama's commitment to accountability ensured that government funds were used efficiently, setting a precedent for ethical governance in the region. He believed that true progress was not just about launching projects but about creating systems that could sustain themselves beyond his tenure. By the end of his third term, Gangakhed had evolved into a more self-reliant constituency, where communities played an active role in maintaining and expanding their own development.

Mama's third term was not just about expanding past successes but about embedding resilience into Gangakhed's growth. His leadership reinforced that meaningful change does not come from one-time projects but from sustained, grassroots-driven initiatives that continuously evolve to meet the needs of the people.

Relationships with Political Luminaries

Sitaram "Mama" Ghandat's rise as an independent and community-focused leader in Gangakhed did not unfold in isolation. Over the decades, he forged close personal and professional ties with many of Maharashtra's and India's most influential figures—people such as Bal Thackeray, Gopinath Munde, Pramod Mahajan, Sharad Pawar, and L. K. Advani, among others. These relationships were not just political transactions; they were often rooted in mutual respect and shaped by Mama's authentic desire to channel powerful connections toward real gains for his constituency. His interactions with these political stalwarts played a significant role in securing aid for development projects, resolving administrative hurdles, and advocating for the welfare of the people of Gangakhed.

Among all his alliances, Mama's rapport with Bal Thackeray, the Shiv Sena founder, stood out for its depth and uniqueness. Thackeray's larger-than-life persona and fiery brand of politics contrasted with Mama's humble, on-the-ground approach, yet the two men found common ground in their devotion to Maharashtra's well-being. Thackeray recognized that Mama had become an influential figure by building true grassroots support, a rarity in politics often dominated by star power or big-party machinery. Impressed by Mama's 1995 independent victory, Thackeray offered him moral backing and, famously, once proposed a ministerial role. Mama's refusal of that cabinet position on the grounds of limited formal education struck Thackeray as a sign of rare humility. It deepened their personal bond, and Thackeray privately praised Mama as "the people's leader" who was unconcerned with personal prestige.

Mama also assisted orphans and Sena staffers who found themselves in dire straits. Sometimes these individuals reached out to Mama's networks, hoping for small scholarships, job referrals, or connections to better facilities. Recognizing Mama's sincerity, Thackeray often deferred to him on how best to distribute resources for humanitarian causes, especially in Marathwada or among SC communities. Where Thackeray's broad political reach provided the funds or approvals, Mama identified families or wards that needed those resources most. Though Mama remained an independent, he accepted Sena's logistical help when it aligned with Gangakhed's interests. For instance, Thackeray might expedite an official letter if Mama's irrigation schemes were delayed due to bureaucratic red tape. In turn, Mama demonstrated unwavering loyalty to Thackeray by participating in major Sena events like the immersion of Masaheb (Meenatai Thackeray's) ashes while continuing to honor his own constituency's inclusive ethos.

During the 1990s and early 2000s, Gopinath Munde and Pramod Mahajan rose to prominence in the BJP, helming various state and national strategies. Mama's own journey had intersected with these leaders in complicated ways, from a tense period where they refused to grant him a BJP ticket in 1995 to occasional behind-the-scenes coordination to support development in Gangakhed. In the mid-1990s, Mama openly criticized Munde and Mahajan's decision to deny him the BJP nomination, an episode that led him to contest and win as an independent. Despite this rocky start, Mama recognized that bridging relationships with these powerbrokers would ultimately help his constituency. Over time, their mutual acquaintances orchestrated dialogues. Munde and Mahajan, though they had once been cautious about Mama's "outsider" approach, could not ignore his repeated electoral success. They began to see Mama less as a rebel and more as an influential MLA with a proven grassroots record.

Mama's relationship with Munde and Mahajan evolved into one of practical cooperation. In one instance, Mama approached Mahajan's office with an urgent plea for orphaned children in a remote area of Gangakhed. Mahajan agreed to help expedite a special grant or connect them with philanthropic backers. Mama's direct request bypassed typical party ranks, demonstrating how his influence cut across party lines. Additionally, Mama sometimes recommended promising local activists for BJP's district committees, ensuring that dedicated workers, regardless of past political differences, found ways to align with the party's mainstream. His endorsements often carried weight, as Mahajan and Munde valued Mama's read of local talents. Even though Mama stayed independent, Munde and Mahajan occasionally assisted him in acquiring state government clearances for specific projects, such as bridging the Godavari or funding particular welfare schemes. Their influence within the administration expedited files that might have languished otherwise. This cooperative dynamic illustrated Mama's pragmatic stance that political differences did not preclude forging alliances for the sake of Gangakhed's progress.

Sharad Pawar, a towering figure in Maharashtra's political sphere, commanded diverse alliances over decades, heading the Nationalist Congress Party and often playing a kingmaker role. Mama's connections to Pawar underscored his willingness to collaborate with any leader capable of uplifting his constituency. Acknowledging Pawar's sway over state-level resources, particularly in agriculture, cooperative banking, and irrigation, Mama engaged him in purposeful dialogues. If a large sugarcane factory or farmers' cooperative in Gangakhed needed special approvals, Mama sometimes appealed directly to Pawar. Pawar, known for supporting cooperative movements, appreciated Mama's track record with Abhyudaya Bank and micro-finance. This mutual respect facilitated occasional policy support or early clearance for new cooperative-based projects in Gangakhed. Observers noted that Mama's knack for bridging gaps aligned well with Pawar's talent for forging cross-party deals. In behind-the-scenes anecdotes, Mama recommended or endorsed local leaders who sought NCP's support for district-level boards. The synergy let Gangakhed tap into government funds or departmental budgets more smoothly.

One widely circulated story involved Mama approaching Pawar to help establish a well-equipped orphanage or children's shelter. Pawar responded by guiding Mama toward relevant state grants. Mama's sincerity convinced Pawar to expedite the paperwork, culminating in a home that still housed vulnerable children. This anecdote revealed how Mama's cross-party ties extended beyond simple election-time alliances. On matters of humanitarian urgency, top leaders recognized Mama's genuine commitment and responded promptly.

Mama's independent identity did not stop him from forging ties at the national level. L. K. Advani, as a senior BJP figure and former Deputy Prime Minister, personified the party's core ideological framework. Though Mama had parted ways with the BJP in terms of formal membership, their paths crossed due to Mama's continued prominence in state politics. On certain political tours to Maharashtra, Advani's team invited Mama to share a stage or partake in smaller dialogue sessions on rural empowerment. Although Mama's direct link to BJP had frayed, his knowledge of cooperative models and local breakthroughs in SC constituencies intrigued BJP's national strategists. Mama used these opportunities to highlight Gangakhed's successes, like bridging the Godavari or upgrading schools, and to press for additional central schemes that might amplify rural progress.

Sometimes, Mama discovered BJP staffers at the constituency level or from other areas who faced personal struggles, such as medical emergencies or family crises. Mama intervened, connecting them with supportive networks or philanthropic channels. Word of these quiet acts traveled back to Advani, reinforcing Mama's image as a caring figure above partisan lines. Occasionally, Mama leveraged these Advani links to nudge central government agencies, like irrigation boards or road transport departments, over delayed approvals for Gangakhed's expansions. Although Mama remained staunchly independent in elections, these lines of communication ensured that his constituency did not miss out on potential central funds or pilot schemes.

Throughout his political lifespan, marked by independent victories and unwavering devotion to Gangakhed, Mama displayed a rare skill in forging personal, trust-based connections with top leaders irrespective of party affiliation. From Bal Thackeray's paternal camaraderie and Sharad Pawar's cooperative synergy to strategic dialogues with Gopinath Munde, Pramod Mahajan, and even L. K. Advani, Mama nurtured a network that transcended typical ideological boundaries. Behind the scenes, these alliances facilitated crucial resource flows into his constituency, whether in the form of orphan support, farmland irrigation approvals, or improved local leadership training. Mama's success hinged on sincerity, as luminaries recognized that whenever he knocked on their doors, it was to champion real needs, not personal ambition or favoritism.

At the same time, Mama never let these top-level relationships dilute his commitment to the people's interest. His direct appeals for legislative or party support served a single purpose: ensuring that Gangakhed's development agenda did not falter for want of bureaucratic sign-offs or budget releases. This delicate balancing act, bridging various party figures, reaffirmed Mama's identity as a politician anchored in moral empathy rather than alliances for alliance's sake. In essence, Mama's wide-ranging ties with powerful figures illustrate a central truth of his career: while local empowerment formed the bedrock of his success, forging strategic friendships at the top echelons offered pathways for achieving local aims. By appealing to influential offices and seeking swift aid for constituency projects, Mama demonstrated that "independent" need not mean "isolated." Instead, it meant harnessing every available avenue, be it Bal Thackeray's paternal compassion, Sharad Pawar's cooperative ethos, or L. K. Advani's national-level clout, to enrich the lives of ordinary villagers in Gangakhed and beyond.

CHAPTER TWENTY-FOUR

PHILOSOPHY, PERSONALITY, AND IMPACT

Sitaram "Mama" Ghandat's decades of public service—whether as an independent MLA, a leader in cooperative banking, or an advocate for marginalized families—have been defined by humility, inclusivity, and an unwavering commitment to grassroots development. His rejection of ministerial positions and refusal to engage in power-driven politics set him apart in a system where many seek titles and influence. Instead, Mama dedicated himself to hands-on governance, ensuring that the people of Gangakhed, regardless of caste, class, or religion, had direct access to leadership that genuinely worked for their well-being. His philosophy of "Janseva" (service to the people) transcended electoral cycles and party lines, making his legacy one of sincere public service rather than political ambition.

Throughout his career, Mama repeatedly turned down offers for ministerial posts, most notably from Bal Thackeray. He cited his limited formal education, having studied only up to the fourth standard in a rural village, as a reason for staying close to the ground rather than assuming responsibilities that required legislative policymaking at the state level. He believed that ministerial duties would demand extensive time in Mumbai, away from the everyday struggles of his constituents. Instead of overseeing large bureaucratic portfolios, he preferred to work directly with people, visiting villages, inspecting roads and irrigation projects, and personally ensuring that welfare measures reached those in need. His choice to remain a people's leader rather than a political figurehead was rare and won him immense respect from both political elites and ordinary citizens alike.

Mama's humility was not performative but deeply ingrained in his leadership style. He rejected the privileges often associated with political office, preferring simple transport and refusing lavish accommodations. Even as an MLA, he maintained a direct, personal approach to problem-solving, often standing in queues with villagers or traveling by ordinary means to experience their challenges firsthand. His belief was that leadership was about moral authority rather than hierarchical power. People trusted him not because of his position but because he remained accessible, consistent, and sincere in addressing their concerns. This was evident even when he was out of office after the 2004 elections—his engagement with the community never wavered, and he continued to work for their development despite lacking a formal title.

Mama's philosophy of "Janseva" extended to his inclusive vision for development. In Gangakhed, where caste divisions historically influenced governance and resource distribution, he worked tirelessly to break barriers and unite communities. His projects, whether roads, irrigation schemes, or educational institutions, were designed to benefit all castes and social groups equally. He formed multi-caste committees to oversee local projects, ensuring that no single group dominated decision-making. By prioritizing fairness in the allocation of government resources, he challenged deeply ingrained biases and fostered a sense of shared responsibility among different communities.

His efforts to promote inclusivity were not limited to governance structures but extended to social and cultural initiatives as well. He actively supported and organized free group weddings, an initiative aimed at reducing the financial burden of marriage ceremonies for low-income families. These weddings brought together couples from different castes and faiths, symbolizing a break from social divisions that had long defined rural Maharashtra. Similarly, his healthcare initiatives, such as mobile medical camps and improved rural clinics, ensured that even the most marginalized groups had access to basic medical care. Mama's focus was always on equal access—whether it was water pipelines, school expansions, or public welfare programs, he ensured that benefits reached everyone, not just the politically influential.

Beyond large-scale projects, Mama's leadership had a deeply personal impact on individuals. His ability to recognize and nurture potential in people from all backgrounds transformed many lives. One widely known story is that of a young hotel waiter who, due to financial hardship, had abandoned his dreams of further education. Mama, recognizing his dedication and intelligence, intervened by helping him secure a job at Abhyudaya Bank. Over time, the young man rose through the ranks, eventually becoming a branch manager. This single act of mentorship not only changed one individual's life but also uplifted his entire family and community, proving that opportunities, when directed toward the right individuals, could create lasting change.

Another example of his impact was in women's empowerment. In a remote hamlet, Mama identified a group of unemployed women skilled in tailoring but lacking financial support. With his help, they secured microloans and access to a cooperative that provided sewing machines and small contracts for school uniforms and other garments. Over time, this group became self-sufficient, earning a stable income that improved their households' financial stability. Mama's involvement did not end at funding; he regularly visited them, offering guidance on quality control, marketing strategies, and expansion opportunities. These women, who once relied on seasonal labor, found economic independence through his encouragement and support.

His intervention was also crucial in emergency situations. In one incident, a pair of accident victims in a rural area lacked immediate medical aid due to the absence of trauma facilities. Mama personally arranged an ambulance and coordinated with a charitable organization to cover their treatment costs. His swift action ensured that the victims received timely medical care, preventing severe long-term consequences. Such interventions, though not widely publicized, reinforced his reputation as a leader who was present in moments of crisis, offering not just political solutions but human empathy.

The impact of Mama's leadership extended beyond his direct actions. His philosophy of service influenced the broader political culture of Gangakhed. Historically, rural politics had been shaped by feudal power structures and caste-based vote banks. Mama's success demonstrated that genuine service and moral integrity could override these divisions. As a result, expectations from politicians in the region changed—leaders were now expected to be more engaged with the people rather than functioning as distant power brokers. Even his political rivals had to adapt, recognizing that voters had come to demand accessibility, transparency, and accountability.

Mama's focus on grassroots empowerment also created a lasting institutional change. By promoting local committees to oversee development projects and public welfare initiatives, he ensured that governance was not entirely dependent on individual leaders. These structures continued to function effectively even when he was not in office, proving that his impact was not just personal but systemic. This decentralized approach reduced reliance on political cycles, enabling sustained development efforts independent of electoral outcomes.

Looking ahead, sustaining Mama's legacy requires institutionalizing his methods and philosophies. One way to do this is by documenting his governance model, highlighting how transparent budgeting, local participation, and inclusive policies contributed to Gangakhed's transformation. There have been discussions about establishing a leadership training program inspired by his principles, aimed at equipping young activists and aspiring public servants with the skills and ethical grounding needed for effective grassroots leadership. Mama himself remains committed to mentoring the next generation, ensuring that his legacy is carried forward through capable individuals who share his dedication to service.

Another challenge is ensuring that as Gangakhed modernizes, the values of accessibility and inclusivity remain intact. With increasing urbanization and economic changes, there is a risk that new political actors may prioritize large-scale investments while neglecting direct engagement with the people. Mama's role as a moral compass for the region will be crucial in maintaining a governance style that prioritizes community-driven development over top-down policymaking.

Sitaram "Mama" Ghandat's impact is not defined by the number of terms he has served or the offices he has held but by the transformation he has brought to the lives of countless individuals. His philosophy of humility, his rejection of personal power for the sake of genuine service, and his unwavering commitment to inclusive development have reshaped both governance and social structures in Gangakhed. His leadership is a testament to the idea that true power lies not in ministerial positions or political influence but in the ability to uplift those in need and create sustainable, community-driven progress.

By integrating political connections with grassroots involvement, Mama set a precedent that challenges the traditional norms of leadership. His ability to bring together powerful figures like Bal Thackeray, Sharad Pawar, and L. K. Advani for the benefit of his people while maintaining a direct, personal relationship with his constituency exemplifies a rare balance in public service. His story is not just about political success but about redefining what it means to be a leader—one who walks alongside the people rather than governing from above. As politics continues to evolve, Mama's legacy stands as a reminder that real progress is measured not in policies alone, but in the lived experiences of those whose lives have been uplifted through genuine, empathetic leadership.

CHAPTER TWENTY-FIVE

LEGACY

The life of Sitaram "Mama" Ghandat is a testament to perseverance, service, and the power of grassroots leadership. From humble beginnings as the son of a cobbler in a small village to becoming a three-time Independent MLA and a significant figure in the cooperative banking sector, his journey reflects an unwavering commitment to public service. His story is not only about political success or achievements in infrastructure; it is about the impact of genuine, people-centric leadership and the ability to transform lives through humility, hard work, and integrity.

Mama's early years were filled with hardship and struggle. Born into a family engaged in traditional boot-making, he faced financial challenges and social limitations from a young age. Despite having only primary education, he never allowed the lack of formal education to restrict his aspirations. Working first as a cobbler and later as a taxi driver in Mumbai, he toiled tirelessly, gaining firsthand experience of the struggles faced by the working class. These early years fostered a deep empathy for common people and fueled his desire to bring about meaningful change for those who faced systemic obstacles like he had.

His entry into politics was unconventional and driven by a sense of duty rather than ambition. Running as an independent candidate, he disregarded party politics and traditional election strategies, focusing instead on direct communication with the people. His first victory in 1995 was a historic moment, proving that genuine connections with voters could triumph over the financial and organizational strength of political parties. His subsequent re-election in 1999 and victorious return in 2009, despite having shifted to the Gangakhed constituency, demonstrated the strength of his grassroots support and his ability to unite communities beyond caste and party lines.

Mama's work was characterized by his consistent focus on development. He did not view politics as a platform for personal gain but as a means of uplifting the people. His efforts in critical areas such as road construction, water supply, electricity distribution, healthcare, and education were aimed not only at development but at enhancing the quality of life for the people. His initiatives in irrigation transformed agricultural productivity in Gangakhed, ensuring that farmers were no longer entirely dependent on unpredictable monsoons. Through cooperative banking, he advanced the process of financial inclusion, providing financial services to thousands of people who had been excluded from the traditional banking system.

Under his leadership of the Abhyudaya Bank, he expanded the bank's branches, creating employment opportunities for thousands. Education was another cornerstone of Mama's vision. By expanding the Abhyudaya Education High School, he provided educational opportunities to more than seven thousand students. His efforts to ensure quality education for marginalized communities were aimed at breaking the cycle of poverty and caste-based discrimination.

The social initiatives started under his leadership provided support to countless families. During the COVID-19 pandemic, he distributed sanitizers, masks, and essential supplies to the poor and working-class people. He made significant financial contributions from his own family's resources towards these efforts. Additionally, he organized free bride and groom introduction events in various cities across Maharashtra, helping many couples find suitable matches.

In March 2025, Sitaram "Mama" Ghandat officially joined the Bharatiya Janata Party (BJP). This decision marked an important milestone in his political journey. His political journey had begun with the Jana Sangh, and now, by formally joining the BJP, he completed a full circle in his political career. This decision is considered a tribute to his work and service, as his independence had made his contributions and service truly recognized. With this entry, his influence is expected to grow even further, allowing him to work on a broader platform through the BJP. The humility and integrity with which he has served will ensure that his legacy reaches future generations.

Inspired by the work of Sitaram "Mama" Ghandat, Sanjay Khamkar and his associates established the 'Loknete Ma. Aamdar Sitaramji Ghandat (Mama) Samajik Pratisthan' in 2014. This foundation has implemented various initiatives for education, employment, healthcare, women empowerment, and marginalized communities. Particularly, efforts were made for women empowerment through the establishment of self-help groups providing employment opportunities. A free accident insurance scheme was launched for artisans and workers. These efforts aimed at the economic progress and empowerment of society continue to prove their importance even today. The foundation has successfully brought communities together through various social initiatives, establishing a sense of social justice and equality.

The value of Mama's work is not limited to his tangible achievements. He introduced a new standard to the political culture of Gangakhed. With simplicity, honesty, and a people-centric approach, he established new ideals in politics. His real recognition lies among the people. This is his true success, and this legacy will continue to endure. His work has inspired many within the community and continues to guide new directions.

Now, as we reach the end of this book, it can be said with certainty that the legacy of Sitaram "Mama" Ghandat's leadership and achievements will continue to flourish and inspire generations to come.